T0358723

Writing up Quantitative Research in the Social and Behavioral Sciences

TEACHING WRITING

Volume 6

Writing up Quantitative Research in the Social and Behavioral Sciences

Marianne Fallon
Central Connecticut State University, USA

SENSE PUBLISHERS
ROTTERDAM/BOSTON/TAIPEI

A C.I.P. record for this book is available from the Library of Congress.

ISBN: 978-94-6300-607-1 (paperback)
ISBN: 978-94-6300-608-8 (hardback)
ISBN: 978-94-6300-609-5 (e-book)

Published by: Sense Publishers,
P.O. Box 21858,
3001 AW Rotterdam,
The Netherlands
https://www.sensepublishers.com/

All chapters in this book have undergone peer review.

Printed on acid-free paper

ADVANCE PRAISE FOR
WRITING UP QUANTITATIVE RESEARCH IN THE SOCIAL AND BEHAVIORAL SCIENCES

"Fallon brings much-needed accessibility to the daunting world of quantitative methods. Filled with contemporary references to pop culture—including sports, music, and television—key concepts are creatively introduced. Succinct, humorous, and thoughtfully organized, *Writing up Quantitative Research in the Social and Behavioral Sciences* breaks the mold for teaching novice researchers how to effectively communicate their work."
– Diana Cohen, Associate Professor of Political Science, Central Connecticut State University

"This book covers the 'how to' of writing research projects in a highly engaging manner. Graduate students who are preparing to work on their master's thesis will get a lot out of this book. Undergraduates doing a thesis or a capstone project will also find this book very helpful. Instructors teaching research methods in the social sciences will find this book makes a useful course companion."
– Damon Mitchell, Professor of Criminology and Criminal Justice, Central Connecticut State University

"Many college students have scarce opportunities to practice professional writing, especially research projects involving data analysis. This text will be a very helpful resource for undergraduate and graduate students in the social and behavioral sciences that need to complete such writing assignments. Using an intuitive and humorous approach, the author provides valuable advice on writing up statistical results across different disciplines; however, the author also dispenses much needed wisdom on how to approach the completion of a large written project, including the avoidance of procrastination and the importance of revision. Modern research often involves working with others trained in disciplines different from one's own. Social and behavioral scientists working on interdisciplinary research teams will also find this book very helpful."
– Brian Osoba, Associate Professor of Economics, Central Connecticut State University

"Kudos to Fallon for writing a very thorough and readable foundational text for beginning researchers! Fallon's inclusion of humor, relatable examples, and conversational style invites students to face their fears as they embark on their early forays into research. In addition to providing a step-by-step guide to preparing and writing a manuscript, students are provided with the tools to think more positively about their personal abilities. The inclusion of information about Dweck's *Mindset* theory as well as the findings of Tough regarding the role of character in being successful in one's endeavors offer students cognitive tools to approach the task. My personal favorite is Chapter 3, because it provides what I've never seen in another textbook—the actual process of writing. The myths, the rules, and the bare hand approach address the foundational issues of writing that interfere with the ability to write anything. The examples of actual student papers at the end of the text provide students the opportunity to examine the work their peers rather than the work of more experienced scholars. I will definitely recommend this text to my colleagues who teach writing and research courses!"
– **Linda Behrendt, Associate Professor of Human Development and Family Studies, Indiana State University**

"I teach a research course for undergraduate seniors where they need to write an APA-style research report. Fallon conveys challenging concepts in a clear, meaningful, and engaging manner. The review of methods and statistics at the beginning of the text is particularly useful and the advice offered to emerging writers is extremely helpful and will encourage those struggling to improve. The examples throughout the book are outstanding; they are relevant, descriptive, and varied. The sample papers are excellent models for emerging researchers navigating their first report."
– **Caitlin Brez, Assistant Professor of Psychology, Indiana State University**

"*Writing up Quantitative Research in the Social and Behavioral Sciences* is not your typical book. It is a MUST HAVE handbook for students in the social and behavioral sciences, laying out a clear review of the research process, hints for success, tips for good writing, and excellent examples of outstanding student papers in several different areas. Faculty in psychological science, sociology, economics, criminology, political science, and communications need this text for their students!"
– **Carolyn Fallahi, Professor of Psychological Science, Central Connecticut State University**

*To my husband, Martin, who helps me chase my dreams
and catch them.*

TABLE OF CONTENTS

PREFACE

When I began writing this book, I – somewhat naively – expected that anything I read about the process of writing would transcend disciplinary boundaries. Good writing is good writing, right? I quickly found that prescriptions vary widely, even across quite accomplished writers. Case in point: Examine the following suggestions for when one should start writing a research report or which section should be tackled first.

> The conventional view of the research process is that we first derive a set of hypotheses from a theory, design and conduct a study to test these hypotheses, analyze the data to see if they were confirmed or disconfirmed, and then chronicle this sequence of events in the journal article... the best journal articles are informed by the actual empirical findings from the opening sentence. Before writing your article, then, you need to analyze your data... Think of your dataset as a jewel. Your task is to cut and polish it, to select the facets to highlight, and to craft the best setting for it. Many experienced authors write the results section first. (Bem, 2004, pp. 186–188)

> Don't wait until the research is done to begin writing because writing... is a way of thinking. Be writing all the time, working on a page or two here, a section there. Research *is* writing. (McCloskey, 2000, p. 22)

> Everett Hughes told me, when I was still in graduate school, to write introductions last. 'Introductions are supposed to introduce. How can you introduce something you haven't written yet? You don't know what it is. Get it written and then you can introduce it.' If I do that, I discover that I have a variety of possible introductions available, each one right in some way, each giving a slightly different twist to my thought. I don't have to find the One Right Way to say what I want to say; I have to find out what I want to say... If I write my introductory sentences after I finish the body of my text, the problem of the One Right Way is less compelling. (Becker, 2007, pp. 50–51)

Bem is a psychologist, McCloskey an economist, and Becker a sociologist.

As an emerging researcher, hearing that there isn't One Right Way may not be comforting. You're probably reading this book precisely because you hoped it would demystify the process of writing a quantitative research report (or your professor made you). You want A Way. *Any* Way. This book offers you A Way – actually Several Ways. You see, I do not believe in One Right Way either.

I do, however, believe in Your Way. That's what you're searching for, isn't it? To be clear, Your Way still needs to conform to discipline-specific guidelines. (This isn't the Wild West.) Your Way still needs to demonstrate a command of the relevant knowledge and a healthy dose of critical thinking. (This is University.) And Your Way still needs to embrace the rules and practices of good writing. (This is good. Period.)

My job, as I see it, is to help you develop Your Way. In that spirit I will share My Way and Other People's Ways. Then you can amalgamate those suggestions into Your Way, which becomes Your Voice.

Many people helped me prepare this book. In particular, I would like to thank my colleagues from departments across the social and behavioral sciences for sharing their time, insight, and students' work. Dr. Brian Osoba helped me wade through the different approaches to econometrics and economic forecasting. He also turned my attention to McCloskey's (2000) work, which should be required reading for any student of social or behavioral science. Dr. Fiona Pearson and Dr. Stephen Adair provided invaluable direction in sociology. Dr. Diana Cohen and Dr. Robbin Smith supplied much needed guidance in Political Science. I also thank Dr. Karen Ritzenhoff for her sage and practical advice.

Special thanks also extend to the students who graciously shared their work and allowed me to edit it for the purposes of this volume: Cory Manento, Anthony Huqui, and Selina Nieves. Thank you for being wonderful and generous emerging researchers.

My immediate and extended family also deserve mention. My husband Martin supplied much needed support, editing, and – above all – time, even when my writing needs compromised his personal goals and fulfillment. My daughters Catherine, Fiona, and Bridget mostly complied when I claimed writing time during their waking hours. My mother and Aunt Mary patiently listened to me talk about this book for over a year and helped me weather the ebbs and flows. A dear family friend, Mary Kennedy, provided editorial assistance.

Finally, I thank Patricia Leavy for affording me the opportunity to develop this book and for the motivation to keep me going. Being a part of this series on *Teaching Writing* is, for me, a celebration of learning and teaching.

INTRODUCTION

This brief, practical, and prescriptive primer will help emerging researchers learn how to write high-quality, quantitative research reports in the social and behavioral sciences. Students from Communications, Criminology or Criminal Justice, Economics, Political Science, Psychological Science, and Sociology will find the suggestions and samples contained herein particularly helpful. Social Work or Education students may also benefit.

I am a psychological scientist and I discuss writing through that lens. Let me explain by way of example: Becker (2007), a sociologist, interprets anxiety over writing through his lens – culturally influenced rituals of writing (e.g., the "right" type of paper, cleaning the house right before writing, etc.). As a psychological scientist, I interpret those behaviors and anxieties as stemming from beliefs about intelligence.

Despite my discipline-specific lens, I have tried to appeal to students across the social and behavioral sciences. I have illustrated concepts with examples from criminology, economics, political science, communications, sociology, and social work. Many examples are interdisciplinary.

I wrote this book with the assumption that you have a working-level knowledge of discipline-relevant research methodology and statistical terms. That said, I elaborated on key methodological and statistical concepts that are critical underpinnings for writing a strong quantitative report. My goal is not to teach you how to conduct quantitative research, but to illustrate how to effectively communicate a research project.

The book is divided into three major sections. The first section provides foundational elements of quantitative research that apply across disciplines. Chapters 1 and 2 review key methodological and statistical concepts. Chapter 3 focuses on discipline-transcendent writing strategies and practices.

The second section details the questions researchers answer within a quantitative research report. These questions cohere around four major themes:

- What question did you ask?
- What did you do to answer your question?
- What did you find?
- What do your findings mean?

Strategies for answering these questions appear in Chapters 4 through 7. Chapter 8 provides information about citations and bookending reports with supporting materials, including a title page, abstract, references, tables and figures, and appendices.

Despite similarities in the overarching questions social and behavioral scientists attempt to answer, disciplines go about communicating their answers differently. A one-size-fits-all solution does not exist. Thus, the third and final section of the book includes three abridged, student-generated papers illustrating the most common forms of quantitative research in the social and behavioral sciences: content analyses, investigations using secondary or archival data, and true experiments with primary data collection. All samples involve a single study and are formatted using a style typical of the discipline (e.g., APA, ASA, or APSA). Although the samples are derived from Psychological Science, Sociology, and Political Science, students from other social and behavioral sciences will benefit from their lessons in terms of approach, if not form.

As a final note, I should say something about my sense of humor: It's quirky and infused throughout the book. Some critics argue that humor detracts from academic writing and trivializes the significance of the work. I choose to take my cue from Deidre McCloskey (2000):

A writer must entertain if she is to be read. Only third-rate scholars and C students are so worried about the academic pose that they insist on their dignity. (p. 43)

FOUNDATIONS FOR WRITING QUANTITATIVE RESEARCH REPORTS IN THE SOCIAL AND BEHAVIORAL SCIENCES

Imagine you are playing a baseball or softball game for the first time. Prior to this moment, you've learned the vocabulary of the game – strike, double-play, infield fly, ground-rule double. You've also learned how to make decisions including how hard to throw the ball or whether to swing at a pitch. You've internalized the rules that govern the game. And you have likely experienced emotional ups and downs during your practice sessions. You may have had to push through frustrating practice, be hopeful that the next practice will get better, and focus your attention to learn effectively. In short, before you take the field or step up to the plate, you've developed a foundation to prepare you for the game.

This section will provide you with the foundation needed to write a research report based on quantitative methods. Chapters 1 and 2 reacquaint you with your equipment and decision-making tools – the methodological and statistical concepts critical to communicating quantitative research intelligently and professionally. Although you have likely encountered these concepts in your Research Methods and/or Statistics courses, some additional practice won't hurt.

Chapter 3 addresses the art of writing well. You need to understand rules that enable high-quality writing. But you also need to consider the emotional and motivational aspects of writing – the "ups and downs" and the "heart" required to succeed. This chapter strikes a balance between the cognitive and emotional underpinnings of solid writing.

METHODOLOGICAL ELEMENTS OF QUANTITATIVE RESEARCH

INTRODUCTION

Returning to the ball game analogy, what would happen if your coach told you to bunt and you forgot what that meant? If you don't know the terminology, you can't play the game well.

When you designed and conducted your research project, you took abstract concepts and put them into practice. Writing about your research project requires an even deeper level of application. Now you must explicitly communicate your project using the terminology of social and behavioral science. This chapter will help you review the methodological concepts most critical to writing a strong research report.

First we distinguish methodological forms of quantitative research that you are most likely to conduct as an emerging researcher. Next we describe an organizational framework to help you understand how you move from abstract constructs to aligned variables and concrete definitions. To bolster confidence using the lexicon of quantitative research, we pay special attention to the different ways we label variables. We conclude with validity and reliability to enable you to interrogate your own and others' research thoroughly and critically.

FORMS OF QUANTITATIVE RESEARCH

In a nutshell, quantitative research is a "top-down" process. You begin with a question. For example: Can you make people believe that they committed a crime when they did not (Shaw & Porter, 2015)? You then examine theories that provide potential explanations for that phenomenon (Kerlinger, 1979). Based on theory, you make predictions and develop a methodology that evaluates those hypotheses. You obtain and analyze data that can be numerically quantified and statistically analyzed (Creswell, 2014). As a final step, you carefully deduce conclusions from your statistical analysis.

Quantitative researchers examine basic, applied, or translational research questions. Basic research involves generating knowledge to understand fundamental processes and mechanisms that do not necessarily apply to real-world problems. For example, psychological scientists might ask how the brain reorganizes motor control after someone experiences a stroke. That information may not directly help stroke victims, but we gain knowledge about the brain's neuroplasticity. Applied research addresses a specific, real-world problem. Sociologists might attempt to identify factors related to increases in the availability and use of opioids (e.g., heroin) in rural areas. Translational research bridges the gap between basic and applied research – you use the knowledge from basic research to develop and test solutions to real-world problems. Economists may take basic research examining increases in healthcare funding in the US and apply it directly to a healthcare access crisis in a specific region or district in the US. No matter the type of research, all questions are grounded in theory and are answered through quantitative analysis.

Quantitative researchers employ several methodologies to obtain data. We will focus on the three most common approaches among emerging researchers: content analysis, primary data collection, and secondary data analysis.

Content Analysis

Content analysis involves carefully examining artifacts that function as a medium for communication (Neuman, 2011), including songs, sculptures, graphic designs, comic strips, newspaper articles, magazine advertisements, books, films, television shows, tweets, instagram pictures, letters, and much more.[1] Quantitative content analysis requires counting the occurrence or rating the strength of particular social or behavioral phenomena within the media. For example, Harold Zullow (1991) examined over three decades of popular song lyrics for "pessimistic ruminations", which involve dwelling on the notion that negative events will persist far into the future and will negatively impact endeavors (Zullow, Oettigen, Peterson, & Seligman, 1988). Pessimistic ruminations within popular songs predicted changes in consumer optimism, which consequently predicted economic growth. So, the more pessimistic songs were, the less optimistic people were about their financial affairs, which stilted the economy. (Anyone want to bet that pessimistic ruminations in songs by Taylor Swift and Katy Perry predict the length of adolescents' romantic relationships?)

Primary Data Collection

Primary data collection occurs *in vivo* (i.e., happening within a living organism). Collecting primary data involves directly obtaining responses from people. Emerging researchers collect such data using a combination of survey, experimental, and observational methods.

A survey approach involves participants completing questionnaires in person or online. For example, Tice and Baumeister (1997) examined whether procrastination was related to physical health symptoms. Undergraduates completed a questionnaire measuring procrastination and physical health symptoms the beginning of the semester. They reported physical health symptoms again at the end of the semester. Procrastinators exhibited fewer health symptoms at the beginning of the semester than did non-procrastinators. However, procrastinators exhibited a 7-fold increase in physical health symptoms by the end of the semester compared to a 2-fold increase in non-procrastinators! (In case you're wondering, procrastination was negatively associated with grades, too.)

An experimental approach attempts to establish a cause-and-effect relationship between phenomena. Researchers systematically manipulate participants' experiences, control extraneous variables, and then measure the outcome. Although experiments are usually conducted in the laboratory, researchers also perform them in natural environments using observational methods. For example, Goddard, Kahn, and Adkins (2015) examined whether pedestrians' race affected how often drivers yielded to pedestrians at a crosswalk. Unobtrusive observers recorded how many cars passed through a crosswalk without stopping for Black or for White pedestrians and how long pedestrians waited to cross. Pedestrians in this study were confederates (i.e., people experimenters employ to play a particular role in a study). They were dressed identically (button-down shirt and khakis) and acted comparably when attempting to cross the street. Drivers yielded for White pedestrians twice as often as they yielded for Black pedestrians. Further, Black pedestrians had to wait approximately 32% longer than White pedestrians to cross the intersection, suggesting that racial bias manifests in a host of everyday events.

Secondary or Archival Data Analysis

Quantitative researchers do not have to collect their own data; other researchers have developed large-scale databases, which can provide fertile ground for testing predictions. For example, Rippeyoung and Noonan (2012) drew data from the National Longitudinal Survey of Youth (NLSY) to investigate whether mothers who breastfed their infants experienced losses in earnings compared to mothers who did not breastfeed. At 1 year post-partum, women who breastfed their infants over 6 months lost more than double the amount of earnings compared to women who formula-fed or breastfed their infants for shorter durations. So much for breastfeeding not costing anything...[2]

THE DEFINITIONAL HIERARCHY

Hierarchies are powerful organizational strategies. All of nature is hierarchically organized. Remember binominal nomenclature from high school biology (kingdom, domain, order, class, etc.)? Even our bodies are hierarchically organized: systems (e.g., respiratory) are made up of organs (e.g., lungs) comprised of tissues (e.g., alveolar tissue) consisting of cells (whatever those are called; I'm not a physiologist).

The point is, we can use the power of the hierarchy to organize phenomena we investigate in the social and behavioral sciences. Organizing phenomena hierarchically has two important advantages. First, we gain deeper appreciation for how an abstract, general concept can be made more concrete and specific. Second, we ensure that the phenomena of interest align with the way we study them.

Imagine you are examining whether physical brightness is associated with morality. You are likely familiar with the metaphor where light connotes good and dark signals evil. Keeping someone "in the dark" involves deception. Walking "in the light" smacks of virtue. Heroes dress in white, villains in black (no offense to goths... or clergy).

So you have two phenomena, physical brightness and morality, that might relate to each other. These phenomena are abstract, theoretical, and broad. These abstractions are known as *constructs*. They function as theoretical "umbrellas" under which a host of different behaviors, feelings, cognitions, and/or motivations fall.

Morality and physical brightness can manifest in various ways. For physical brightness, you might change the illumination of a room or computer screen or you could ask participants to rate how bright they think the testing room is. We have arrived at the second rung of the hierarchy: the *variable*. The key to understanding variables is to know they can vary, or take multiple values along some sort of dimension or continuum. For example, you could make the room really bright, really dark, or many increments in between. Your variable would be "room illumination".

Making a room "really bright" is vague. If people wanted to replicate your study, they would need to know exactly how bright the room should be. You need to *operationally define* variables in detail. Operational definitions tell readers exactly what you are doing in your study (see Figure 1.1). Perhaps your bright room would be illuminated with a 150-watt bulb and your dim room lit with a 30-watt bulb.

We have now moved completely through the hierarchy. Your construct, physical brightness, varies by room illumination, which is defined as using a 150-watt (high illumination) or 30-watt bulb (low illumination). The hierarchy moves form general to specific and the variables and definitions align with the construct. Note well that each construct of interest forms its own hierarchy. Try generating a definitional hierarchy for morality.

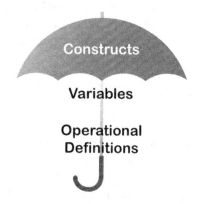

Figure 1.1. Visual schematic of the definitional hierarchy[3]

TYPES OF VARIABLES

Let's linger on the middle rung of the hierarchy. Social and behavioral scientists label variables based on their methodological function. This terminology is challenging to master, but essential for understanding your project and communicating it clearly and accurately. We begin with the most basic methodological distinction: measured and manipulated variables. We extend our discussion to extraneous variables that could affect the relationship between your measured and/or manipulated variables of interest.

Measured and Manipulated Variables

Measured variables document behavior, attitudes, or physical characteristics. You can measure variables through self-report (e.g., a questionnaire), behavioral observation (e.g., amount of eye contact during a speech), or physiological recording (e.g., heart rate). If your study contains only measured variables, you are likely examining associations or predictive relationships between variables. In such cases, researchers specify *predictor* variables that account for variation in an *outcome* variable. All studies have measured variables; only some studies have manipulated variables.

Manipulated variables are researcher-engineered, systematic experiences designed to investigate a causal relationship. Manipulating one or more variables (i.e., independent variables) causes a change in a measured variable (i.e., dependent variable). You can manipulate variables externally (e.g., change an economic incentive for completing a task) or internally (e.g., induce feelings of gratitude by asking people to count their blessings). Researchers further distinguish manipulations on the basis of how participants experience conditions. If participants experience only one condition, the manipulation is *between participants*. If participants experience all conditions, the manipulation is *within participants*.

Extraneous Variables

Extraneous variables are, frankly, nuisances. Whereas measured and manipulated variables are central to your predictions and analysis, extraneous variables are peripheral. They merit attention because of their potential impact on the relationship between your variables of interest. Let's say you are analyzing episodes of *The Walking Dead* for hopeful, uplifting words or actions (good luck). You surmise that earlier seasons contain more hopeful content than later seasons (because the zombie apocalypse has a knack for bringing people down). An extraneous variable could be the number of episodes in a season. Season 1 has considerably less content to analyze than later seasons. Another extraneous variable is the rapidity with which main characters exit the show and fringe characters become central.

Extraneous variables are also problematic for studies involving direct data collection. Imagine you examine how watching violent media affects people's perceptions of others. One group of participants watches a film containing gratuitous violence and another group watches a film containing violence necessary for survival. Then, participants complete a questionnaire regarding how much they like the experimenter. To ensure that the content of the videos changes person perception, you would present the media for the same amount of time, dress in the same way for all participants, keep the volume of the films similar, ask participants with imperfect vision to wear their glasses or contacts while watching the media, etc. Researchers address anticipated extraneous variables by holding them constant, or not allowing them to vary.

Sometimes extraneous variables occur unexpectedly. A loud noise could distract your participants. A participant may have eaten three plates of beans before arriving at your study. These situations are unfortunate and could increase variability in participants' responses. But at least the events occur inconsistently (let's hope) and thus affect your data unsystematically.

You have a serious problem when an extraneous variable varies systematically across conditions of an independent variable. Imagine that you tested participants who watched the violence-for-survival video in a spacious, comfortable classroom and participants who experienced the gratuitous-violence video in a hot, cramped classroom. In other words, you confounded exposure to violence with the testing environment. Lo and behold, participants who watched gratuitous violence reported less favorable perceptions of the experimenter than those who saw violence to survive. You can't be confident that exposure to a certain type of violence explains a person's perception. Suffering in a less-than-optimal testing environment could just as easily account for the finding. Sadly, confounds are terminal – there's no methodological or statistical cure.

VALIDITY AND RELIABILITY

Your and others' confidence in your findings depend upon the validity and reliability of your methods and results. In your research report, you will critically evaluate whether your study passes muster. According to Morling (2015), understanding four broad forms of validity and three types of reliability will help you interrogate your (and others') findings.

Validity

Put broadly, validity involves making a conclusion or decision that is appropriate, reasonable, accurate, and justifiable (Morling, 2015). In the social and behavioral sciences, there are multiple forms of validity, including external, construct, internal, and statistical validity.

External validity. Your study demonstrates high external validity when your results can reasonably generalize to the larger population from which you drew your sample and to other time periods or similar situations. For example, if you analyzed a sample of 20 of the most popular songs from 2015 for gender stereotypes, would your findings generalize to the population of pop songs from 2015, to R & B songs from 2015, or to pop songs from 2005?

Construct validity. Your study possesses high construct validity when your variables are well aligned with your constructs and your operational definitions are clearly specified (thank you, definitional hierarchy). In other words, your variables and operational definitions manipulate or measure the construct accurately.

Many published questionnaires are rigorously examined for convergent validity, divergent (or discriminant) validity, and/or criterion validity. (Wait – *more* validities? Yep.) Convergent validity establishes that an instrument positively or negatively correlates with – converges with – another questionnaire measuring a theoretically related construct. For example, Martin Seligman (2006) developed a questionnaire that measured one's optimism, which is the belief that good things are on the horizon and that people will ultimately achieve their aspirations (VandenBos, 2015). To determine convergent validity, one could measure dispositional hope (Snyder, 1996). However, convergent validity is like confirmation bias; sometimes we look for evidence that confirms our assertion instead of testing alternatives that disprove it. Thus, researchers do not stop probing once they have evidence for convergent validity.

Researchers also establish divergent validity, which is essentially the opposite of convergent validity. An instrument has divergent validity when scores are not, or quite weakly correlated with a questionnaire measuring an unrelated construct. In our example, one might use an instrument measuring agreeableness to establish divergent validity with the optimism questionnaire. You can be optimistic without being agreeable.

It's one thing to establish construct validity through a slew of self-report questionnaires. Relating scores on an instrument to actual embodiments of the construct powerfully establish a special form of construct validity known as criterion validity. An instrument possesses criterion validity when scores correlate with behaviors or internal states that reflect the construct. Returning to our example, the optimism questionnaire reveals optimism as well as the opposite – pessimism. Pessimism is a defining characteristic of depression (Seligman, 2006). Thus, people who are clinically depressed should score lower on the optimism questionnaire than people who are not (and they do!).

Internal validity. Your study exhibits high internal validity when you are confident that the relationship between two or more variables is not due to another variable. Within the design of your study, you carefully control variables and/or measure variables that might explain the relationship of interest. In short, you methodologically rule out potential alternative explanations for the relationships you observed.

Internal validity is especially critical for true experiments that contain at least one manipulated variable. To convincingly argue that change in one variable causes systematic change in another, researchers must clearly demonstrate that the variation was not likely caused by some extraneous variable, an issue sometimes called the *third-variable problem* or *tertium quid* (Field, 2013). (Who says Latin is a dead language?) To maximize internal validity, researchers randomly assign participants to conditions, or, in the case of within-participant manipulations, vary the order in which participants experience conditions.

Statistical validity. Your study is high in statistical validity when your statistical analysis is appropriate to test your prediction(s) and you have made well-informed conclusions regarding statistical significance (i.e., the probability of obtaining a test statistic that large by chance) and effect size (i.e., the real-world importance of the result). If that last sentence sounded like gobbledygook, you will be thrilled to learn that Chapter 2 contains a brief review of essential statistical concepts.

Reliability

Reliability involves how consistently an instrument or procedure produces the same results. Thus, reliability has implications for construct validity. If a questionnaire or procedure does not produce consistent results, it cannot meaningfully reflect behavior, thought, feeling, or motivation. We will discuss three main types of reliability: inter-item reliability (sometimes called internal consistency), test-retest reliability, and inter-rater reliability.

Inter-item reliability (Internal consistency). Self-report instruments often include multiple questions or items that measure a single construct (or variable). This makes a lot of sense; you would be hard-pressed to demonstrate construct validity in a questionnaire that consists of only one item. Imagine boiling down "well-being" to a single question: *Are you happy?* Constructs are too complex to be pigeonholed.

Consequently, responses to items that measure the same construct should be positively related to each other. So, if participants are indeed feeling good about their life, they should respond consistently to questions about most, if not all characteristics of a good life: being satisfied with life, believing they are achieving their goals, etc.

Test-retest reliability.   Some instruments measure constructs thought to remain relatively stable over time, such as personality or intelligence. To determine whether scores fluctuate, researchers administer their instrument to the same participants at least twice. If an instrument has high test-retest reliability, participants who scored high the first time (relative to the other participants) should score high the next time.

Not all instruments need exhibit high test-retest reliability to prove their utility in quantitative research. Questionnaires that measure transient states (e.g., mood and perceived stress) would be expected to produce scores that vary widely upon retesting. Such instruments are particularly useful as dependent variables in experiments because they are sensitive to momentary fluctuations.

Inter-rater reliability.   This form of reliability is specific to content analysis or studies involving behavioral observations. Fatigue, bias, and practice can easily affect raters' or observers' perceptions and subsequent ratings. To ensure that ratings are reliable, additional observers should rate at least a subset of the content or observations. The greater consistency between observers or raters, the more reliable your data are.

A word of caution.   Putting your project under the microscope can be unnerving and may lead you to wonder whether your study is rubbish. Rest assured, your study has value despite its limitations. No study is perfect. The purpose of interrogating the validity and reliability of your study is to acknowledge its caveats while appreciating the contribution it makes to science and its potential to help people. You can make realistic, well-informed conclusions without trashing your hard work.

SUMMARY AND PRACTICE

We laid important methodological groundwork in this chapter. We reviewed terms essential for effectively communicating quantitative research in the social and behavioral sciences. Put this knowledge to use. Grab a piece of paper or open a new document on your computer. Map out your constructs, variables, and operational definitions. Label your variables. Generate at least four questions about the reliability and validity of your project. There. You just started writing your research report.

NOTES

[1] The traditional function of content analysis is to "make valid inferences from text" (Weber, 1990, p. 9). I present a broader view of content analysis that extends to visual and possibly tactile media.

[2] Another form of secondary data analysis involves meta-analysis whose goal is to provide an accurate estimate of the strength of a relationship or effect. In this method, researchers examine previously published studies and sometimes unpublished data that test the same research question. Then researchers estimate an effect size based on the available research. Although meta-analysis deserves mention, it is a special case of secondary data analysis. Discussing meta-analysis further is beyond the scope of this book.

[3] http://www.clipartbest.com/umbrella-clip-art

CHAPTER 2

STATISTICAL ELEMENTS OF QUANTITATIVE RESEARCH

INTRODUCTION

Back to the game – you're at the plate. Will the next pitch be a fastball? Is this pitch in the strike zone and are you going to swing? Now you're in the field. Should you be satisfied with a force at second or go for a double play? Do you try to pick off the runner on first and risk a balk? Decisions, decisions! Taking action at the plate or in the field requires you to process evidence and make a decision. Simply put, you conduct an internal statistical analysis and act accordingly.

In quantitative research, statistical analysis occurs externally and deliberately. Your analysis allows you to accomplish three important goals. First, you describe your data. Second, you ascertain whether the variables you examined in your sample are likely related in the population. Third, you determine whether the relationships or effects are important.

Developing a solid foundation in statistics helps you ensure that your study has statistical validity (see Chapter 1). We begin by reviewing the quantitative properties of variables and then how to summarize the data using descriptive statistics. We discuss fitting a model to your data, which enables you to determine whether the relationships you observed in your study are likely to be reflected in the population. We conclude by discussing effect size, or the real-world importance of the observed relationship or effect.

QUANTITATIVE PROPERTIES OF VARIABLES

From a statistical perspective, variables can be divided into two broad classes: categorical variables and continuous variables. This distinction influences how you describe data and conduct inferential tests.

Categorical variables distinguish categories or classes. Some categorical variables involve binary distinctions (employed/unemployed, enrolled/not enrolled, bunch/fold). Other categorical variables specify multiple options, none of which are necessarily more or better than another, just different (race, sexual orientation, favorite inmate on *Orange Is the New Black*). A final type of categorical variable involves ordered categories, or ranks. Olympic medalists are a perfect example. In the men's 100-meter dash of the 2012 Olympics, Usain Bolt clocked a stunning 9.63 seconds. The second place finisher, Yohan Blake, lagged more than a tenth of a second behind at 9.75s. The bronze-medalist, Justin Gatlin, was only 4 hundredths of a second slower at 9.79s. And the fourth-place finisher, Tyson Gay, ran 9.80s – nearly indistinguishable from Gatlin! But the magnitude of difference between the ranks is irrelevant; all that matters for a medal is the ranking.

Unlike categorical variables, continuous variables preserve the magnitude of difference between values on the dimension you are measuring. Let's say you wanted to track Usian Bolt's 100-meter time over several years. In this case, you would want a continuous variable as a measure, not a categorical one. Values for continuous variables, in theory, could be extended to any level of precision (assuming you had an extremely sensitive instrument!). So, Bolt's average time across all of his 100-meter races in 2011 might be 9.876453 seconds. Another form of continuous variable is a discrete variable, where a given observation can take only certain values on a dimension. For example, on a 20-item quiz, someone could not answer 10.3874 questions correctly. However, we could conceive of a group of people averaging between 10 and 11 questions correct. Thus, a continuum exists underneath the discrete values representing individual observations or scores (Field, 2013).

DESCRIBING YOUR DATA

Readers hunger for details about the data. Common descriptive statistics include frequencies, measures of central tendency, and measures of dispersion.

Frequencies

Calculating frequencies requires counting the number of occurrences of a category; thus, frequencies are used to report categorical variables. Imagine you are examining whether women are more likely than men to graduate from university in 4 years. You could report the raw number of women and men from the entering undergraduate class of 2011 who graduated in 4 years (e.g., 495 women, 266 men) or percentages (e.g., 65% of students who graduated in 4 years were women). Favor percentages when you have a large-ish sample and the number of members within categories is unequal.

Measures of Central Tendency

Measures of central tendency characterize continuous variables using a single, representative value. Most commonly, researchers report the arithmetic mean, or average of observations or elements in the sample. For example, if you gave participants a questionnaire about perceived stress, you could report the average stress score across all participants.

Another option is to report the median, or "middle" value. To calculate the median, you arrange values of a variable in ascending order and find the midpoint. Medians are particularly useful when you have a skewed distribution where several values extend far above or below the majority of values. Take the base salaries of NFL players in 2015 – most players make between $870,000 and $2,750,000, but a handful (22 to be exact) have base salaries over $10,000,000 per year (http://www.spotrac.com/nfl/rankings/base/). So, if you reported the mean base salary ($2,297,208) you would overestimate what most players make. In this case, the *median* base salary of $1,250,000 is more representative of the entire sample than the mean.

A final measure of central tendency is the mode, or the most frequent value in a sample. The mode is not commonly reported, although it may be particularly relevant if the data in your sample have two or more distinct modes. Imagine you are a pollster assessing constituents' attitudes about a controversial issue in an upcoming local election. You ask respondents to rate their agreement with a proposition on a scale of 1 to 9 with 1 being strongly disagree and 9 being strongly agree. If you find distinct modes at values 3 and 7, you have a polarized electorate.

Measures of Dispersion

Like measures of central tendency, measures of dispersion are also single values that describe distributions of continuous variables. Dispersion statistics capture the sample's variability, or how much individual scores or observations differ from each other. The most commonly reported measure is standard deviation, which reflects the approximate average that any value in a sample deviates (i.e., differs) from the mean of the distribution.

You may be asking yourself: Why do I need to know the standard deviation of a distribution? Isn't the mean (or other measure of central tendency) enough? Nope. Imagine you are in a class of 100 students and your professor tells you that the average grade on the first exam was 80 out of 100. You scored a 90, and you're feeling pretty good about yourself. But you are curious – how many other students scored a 90 or above? That's where knowing the standard deviation can be helpful. Let's say the standard deviation of the class grades is 8 points. Assuming that the grades are distributed normally (i.e., in a bell curve), 95% students earned between 74 and 96 (i.e., 2 standard deviations above and below the mean). Your score of 90 is at the top end of that distribution and four other students probably earned the same grade as you (see Figure 2.1). Roughly 8 students scored better than you. Now, let's cut the standard deviation in half – 4 rather than 8. The average test grade is the same (80) and your grade is still 90. With a smaller standard deviation, your grade is even more impressive; you probably earned the highest grade in the class. Thus, knowing the standard deviation helps you appreciate how individual scores relate to all scores within the distribution.

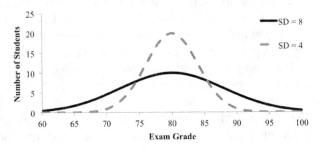

Figure 2.1. Grade distributions with the same mean, but different standard deviations

Measures of dispersion become especially critical when you are comparing different samples, groups, or conditions. Let's say your professor offers your class the opportunity to complete online quizzes in preparation for the upcoming exam. For half of the students ($n = 50$), your professor offers no course credit for completing the quizzes; the other half of students receives extra credit. (Let's not worry about the ethical conundrum this professor now faces.) Students who did not receive credit averaged 75, whereas students who received credit averaged 85. That 10-point difference seems large, but does it reflect a difference in the population? You wouldn't know without examining the standard deviation of the distributions. Imagine the standard deviation is 6, which is reasonably large in this case. Look at Figure 2.2. Many values overlap across the distributions of students who receive or do not receive credit for their quizzes. Thus, the difference between the samples is not likely statistically significant. Although students who receive credit for completing practice quizzes perform better on the exam than students who do not receive credit, this difference may not reflect a difference in the population.

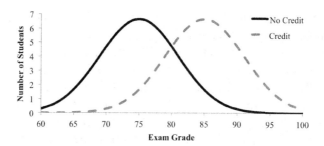

Figure 2.2. Normal distributions that overlap considerably

Now, let's take the same example and halve the standard deviation in both groups to 3 (see Figure 2.3). The mean difference between the groups is the same (still 10 points), but the dispersion has changed. Notice that the curves are narrower and the amount of overlap between the distributions is smaller. The less overlap between distributions, the more likely the difference between the means reflects a real difference in the population. In this case, the difference between students who received credit and those who did not probably reflects a real difference in the population of undergraduate students taking a similar course.

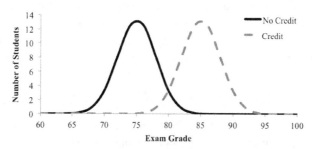

Figure 2.3. Normal distributions that overlap a little

FITTING STATISTICAL MODELS TO YOUR DATA

The goal of your analysis is to fit a statistical model to your data. Nate Silver does this for a living (see http://fivethirtyeight.com/contributors/nate-silver/). He asks interesting questions about sports, politics, economics, and sociology. Then he answers those questions by estimating parameters (e.g., the mean, an unstandardized regression coefficient) and calculating test statistics (e.g., F). Silver is rather good at it; in 2012 he accurately predicted the midterm election winners in all 50 races… even Florida. The title of his book, *The Signal and the Noise* (Silver, 2012), is the perfect metaphor for assessing how your model fits the data.

To assess the fit of your model, you calculate a test statistic that compares the signal (your model) to the noise. Let's break that down. Individual scores or values on your outcome (or dependent) variable differ. Some of that variation is due to factors that you are not directly studying, such as extraneous variables: respondents may be tired, cell phones interrupt a testing session, raters differ slightly in their perceptions of behavior or content, etc. That's noise. But your scores also systematically vary with your predictor (or independent) variables. That's your signal. To compare signal to noise, examine the ratio of systematic variation to unsystematic variation in the outcome variable (Field, 2013).

If you have more signal than noise (or more systematic variation than unsystematic variation), your test statistic will be greater than 1 (see Equation 1).

$$\text{Test statistic} = \frac{\text{signal}}{\text{noise}} = \frac{\text{systematic variation}}{\text{unsystematic variation}} \tag{1}$$

The larger your test statistic, the more variation your model explains (i.e., the better your model fits the data). You can then assess the probability of obtaining a test statistic that large by chance alone using null hypothesis significance testing.

Null Hypothesis Significance Testing (NHST)

Hypotheses are predictions about the phenomena you are studying. Typically, you expect phenomena to be related, which is known as an *alternative* hypothesis. But inferential statistical tests evaluate the *null* hypothesis. "Null" means "zero". Thus, a null hypothesis predicts no relationship between the variables in your study. Let's say you are examining the relationship between dissatisfaction with the current federal government and participation in civic activism. Your alternative hypothesis is that there is a relationship between dissatisfaction with government and civic activism. Your null hypothesis is that there is no relationship between those variables.

Why do we focus on testing the null hypothesis when the alternative hypothesis is really what we are interested in? To answer this question, you need to understand the logic of null hypothesis testing (Field, 2013):

- Assume that the null hypothesis is true (i.e., there is no relationship between variables in the population).
- Fit a statistical model to the data (i.e., calculate a test statistic) and see how much variation it explains in the outcome or dependent variable.
- Determine how well the model fits the data by calculating the probability of obtaining a test statistic as large as you observed if the null hypothesis were true. In other words, if there were no relationship in the population, how likely would it be that you obtained a test statistic that large due to chance alone?
- Make a conclusion about fit: if the probability is small (usually .05 or less), conclude that the model is a good fit. Large test statistics are not likely to occur by chance and therefore inspire confidence that your model accurately reflects the true relationship in the population. In such cases, your finding would be considered *statistically significant*.

The third point is particularly crucial for understanding why we evaluate the null hypothesis rather than the alternative. Think of a courtroom: A defendant is innocent until proven guilty. Similarly, researchers act on the assumption that the null hypothesis is true (the defendant didn't do anything) and the burden of proof involves amassing convincing evidence that the null hypothesis should be rejected (the defendant did something). Imagine what it would be like the other way around: It is much more difficult to prove that someone didn't do *anything* (Privitera, 2015).

When you use NHST, you risk making wrong conclusions. For example, your test statistic may be large enough to conclude that your model is a good fit to the data. But you may have just happened to obtain a large test statistic by chance. It's not that probable, but it is *possible*. If you conclude that your model is a good fit to the data when it is not, you've made a Type I error. Researchers attempt to minimize the likelihood of a Type I error by setting a stringent *alpha level*, the probability that you use to determine whether your model is a good fit to the data. At $\alpha = .05$, 5 times out of 100 you risk claiming that your model accurately reflects the relationship or effect in the population when, in reality, the model does not.

You can imagine the opposite scenario where you conclude that your model is a poor fit to the data, when it actually is a good fit in the population. In this case, you have made a Type II error. The amount of unsystematic variation was too large relative to your systematic variation. Researchers generally assume a maximum Type II error rate (or β level) of .20 (Cohen, 1992). Thus, assuming the relationship actually exists in the population, you run the risk of missing it 20 out of 100, or 1 out of 5 times. See Figure 2.4 for a schematic of these potential outcomes.

		In the population, the relationship…	
		exists	does not exist
Your test statistic is…	large enough to conclude the model is a good fit	CORRECT DECISION!	TYPE I ERROR
	not large enough to conclude that the model is a good fit	TYPE II ERROR	CORRECT DECISION!

Figure 2.4. Potential outcomes of null hypothesis significance testing

Using the common alpha and beta levels, we are more likely to make a Type II error (20%) than a Type I error (5%). Why are scientists generally more "OK" with making a Type II error? Let's work through a real-world example: pregnancy. In reality, someone is or is not pregnant. This is akin to an effect being present or absent in a population. The "test statistic" in this case is a pregnancy test, which is sensitive to the hormone human chorionic gonadotropin (hCG). Based on the concentration of hCG in urine, the test provides a positive result (pregnant) or a negative result (not pregnant). A Type I error occurs when the test produces a positive result when in reality someone is not pregnant (i.e., a false positive). A Type II error arises when the test yields a negative result when someone is actually pregnant (i.e., a false negative). So, can you see why we would rather make a Type II error than a Type I error?

Although Type II errors are generally more concerning than Type I errors, committing a Type I error could produce serious negative consequences in certain circumstances. If you claim that a drug produces an effect when it does not, consumers may endure side effects of the drug without the intended benefit. To the extent that public policy is based on research, municipalities and states could commit taxpayer revenue to projects or initiatives based on a chance finding. The potential consequences of making Type I or II errors emphasize the importance of empirical replication.

Choosing the Appropriate Test Statistic

If all test statistics boil down to finding the signal in the noise, why are there so many statistical tests? Variables differ in their quantitative properties. Different tests are better suited for analyzing categorical and continuous variables. Further, your research question, predictions, and methodology will influence your choice of statistical test. For example, if your goal is to examine how parental political affiliations are related to their children's interest in politics, you might perform ordinary least squares regression on continuous variables. Having at least one categorical outcome variable may point towards a probit or logit regression. To statistically control for extraneous variables, you might conduct a hierarchical regression or ANCOVA.

Providing a detailed discussion of the panoply of statistical tests is beyond the scope of this book. Consult a statistics text, preferably one with a flowchart to help you reason through your options.[1] Your instructor is an invaluable resource as well!

Estimating Error

You've calculated statistics from a sample that *estimate* the true value in the population. Thus, those estimates contain some error (unsystematic variation or noise). We will discuss two ways to estimate error: the standard error of the sample means and confidence intervals.

Standard error is like standard deviation; it estimates average dispersion. But rather than estimating variation among individual points in a sample, standard error reflects the average dispersion of sample means. Imagine you replicated the same study 50 times. The standard error would be the standard deviation for all of those sample means. Standard error helps you determine whether the mean you obtained in your study is likely to be comparable to the population mean (Field, 2013). If the standard error is large, there is a lot of variability between the means of different samples. Therefore, your sample is probably not representative of the population. By contrast, small standard error reflects little difference between sample means, so most means (including yours) should be similar to the true population mean.

Confidence intervals provide boundaries within which the true population mean is thought to fall. Typically, researchers calculate 95% confidence intervals; if you replicated your study 100 times, the true population mean will fall within this interval 95 out of 100 times (Field, 2013). Confidence intervals are particularly useful for comparing sample means across conditions of particular variables. Say you examined whether identifying as politically conservative or liberal was related to a neural response to disgusting images (see Ahn et al., 2014). You recorded blood flow to a part of the brain called the amygdala, which is involved in emotional processing and memory. You found that the neural response to disgusting pictures was greater in participants who self-identified as conservatives compared to those who identified as liberals. But is that difference likely to reflect a true difference in the population? To answer this question, you should construct 95% confidence intervals around the means representing change in blood flow for conservatives and for liberals. Let's say that the intervals do not overlap; that is, the bottom of one interval does not cross the top of the other (see Figure 2.5). Non-overlapping intervals suggest that the samples were drawn from two truly distinct populations – in this case, liberals and conservatives. If the confidence intervals for liberals and conservatives overlapped a fair bit, we would less confident that the means really came from distinct populations (see Figure 2.6). Confidence intervals can be calculated for any statistic, not just sample means.

Confidence intervals correspond to the probability of making a Type I error (Cumming & Finch, 2005). In Figure 2.5, you can see a gap between the lower bound of the 95% CIs for conservatives and the upper bound for liberals. If the boundaries of 95% CIs do not overlap, the probability of making a Type I error is less than .01. Boundaries that barely touch correspond to a p value of approximately .01. Boundaries with moderate overlap (25% of the CI) reflect our typical α-level, .05.

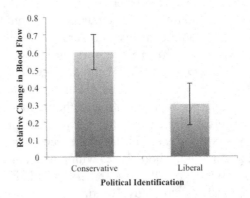

Figure 2.5. Differences between means with non-overlapping confidence intervals

The 95% CIs in Figure 2.6 overlap too much to be considered "statistically significant".

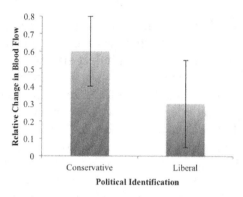

Figure 2.6. The same difference between means, but with larger, overlapping confidence intervals

If CIs inform us about statistical significance, why bother with NHST? Cumming (2014) and others have recently taken up that question and consider NHST irrelevant. However, a good deal of social and behavioral science research has used NHST to draw conclusions. An emerging researcher like yourself should understand how NHST works so you can critically evaluate the statistical validity of the extant literature.

EXAMINING THE STRENGTH OF YOUR MODEL

If we know that a finding is statistically significant, what more is there to discuss? Obtaining statistical significance depends upon having enough statistical power, or the ability the ability to detect a relationship if one actually exists in the population. Thus, statistical power is the inverse of Type II error rate. You can increase statistical power by decreasing the amount of noise, or unsystematic variation in your test statistic. A surefire way to reduce noise is to increase sample size. If your sample is large enough, your model will be statistically significant. But that does not mean your model explains much variation in dependent or outcome variables. You have only reduced unsystematic error enough to pass the threshold for statistical significance.

Consider the other side of the coin. Perhaps your study does not have much statistical power and, because of certain constraints, you cannot obtain more data. You conclude that your model is not statistically significant, but you notice that it accounts for a fair amount of variation in your scores. Thus,

25

the model could be important. Should you ignore this potentially important finding because the model is not statistically significant (but could be with more statistical power)?

Simply put, determining whether a finding is statistically significant is not the whole story. You need to know whether it is important; you need to examine its *effect size*. Broadly stated, effect size is the "size of anything that may be of interest" (Cumming, 2014, p. 34). Technically, the mean or difference between means qualify as effect sizes. But means aren't terribly useful when trying to get a sense of how the phenomenon manifests across multiple contexts. Researchers often investigate the same phenomenon using different methods or measures and means would be reported in the original units of their measurements. So, comparing the magnitude of a finding across studies based on means alone would be difficult. Consequently, we will focus on quantifying effect sizes using methods that do not depend on the original units of measurement.

Some effect size statistics reveal how much variation your independent or predictor variables explain in your dependent or outcome variables. A correlation coefficient is probably the most straightforward example for measuring the proportion of variation one variable explains in another. Correlation coefficients describe the direction and strength of a relationship between two variables. If you square the value of the correlation coefficient, you obtain the proportion of variance one variable accounts for in another. So, let's say you have a correlation coefficient of .10. This value represents a weak, positive relationship. Squaring this value gives you .01, which corresponds to 1% of variance accounted for. Imagine the relationship is strong with a correlation coefficient of .50 (Cohen, 1992). Squaring .5 gives you .25, or 25% of variance accounted for. In behavioral and social research, explaining 25% of the variance is worthy of jumping out of your chair and dancing (your choice of style).

Other statistics quantify effect size in standard deviation units. Cohen's *d*, the most well-known statistic of this nature, is used to compare two means. Without getting into too much detail, Cohen's d tells you how many standard deviations separate the means. Cohen (1992) notes that *d* values of .2, .5, and .8, represent small, medium, and large effects, respectively. One notable advantage of Cohen's *d* is that the statistic does not depend on sample size. That said, the larger your sample, the more likely you are to accurately estimate the means and standard deviations of the population.[2] Thus, larger samples should yield more accurate – not necessarily *larger* – effect sizes.

Pearson *r* coefficients and Cohen's *d* are only two examples of effect size statistics. You can use other effect size metrics depending on the test statistics you calculate.

SUMMARY AND PRACTICE

Statistics help you describe your data and determine whether your findings are statistically significant and important. Grab another piece of paper (physical or digital). Label your dependent or outcome variables as categorical or continuous. List the descriptive statistics that you should report for these variables. State the null hypotheses that you will evaluate. For each null hypothesis, identify the inferential test that you should conduct and corresponding effect size statistic.

After you conduct your analyses for each hypothesis, determine whether your model is a good fit to the data using null hypothesis testing and confidence intervals. Consider the likelihood of making a Type I or Type II error. Examine effect sizes to assess how strong the observed relationship may be in the population. And you have written more of your research report.

NOTES

[1] I recommend Andy Field's *Discovering Statistics* series.

[2] Note carefully that large samples are NOT necessarily representative samples. Depending on how the data are collected, a large sample can still be a biased sample. Mathematically, the larger the sample, the more likely effect sizes will accurately reflect the population. This is a probability, not a certainty.

SUCCESSFULLY WRITING ABOUT QUANTITATIVE RESEARCH (OR ANYTHING)

INTRODUCTION

To successfully play ball, you need to know the rules of the game, how to think like a champion, and have heart. Notice I did *not* mention natural, inborn talent. Clearly, talent helps; but it is not sufficient for success.

That, in a nutshell, is the plot of *Moneyball* (Lewis, 2004). By all accounts Billy Beane was a natural athlete – a guaranteed hall-of-famer. But he did not know how to convert setbacks on the field or at the plate into success and his career as a major league player ended before it began. Once Beane began thinking differently about setbacks, he did quite well as the general manager of the Oakland A's.

Writing bears similarities to softball, baseball, or any complex skill that you want to perform well. You should know the rules of writing and appreciate how your mindset influences your approach to writing. Mindset is the lens through which the rules of good writing make sense. Accordingly, we'll start there.

MINDSET

Fear is perhaps the biggest deterrent to writing well. Becker (2007) asked his students, some of whom were accomplished academic writers, what they were so afraid of. Students feared that their writing would be a disorganized jumble of half-baked ideas. Further, students expected to be mercilessly mocked for writing the "wrong" thing. Sound familiar?

I contend that fears about writing are connected to beliefs about intelligence (i.e., how well you think). Fear arises from this progression of thoughts:

Writing reveals how I think.
Poor writing reflects poor thinking.
Poor thinking equals stupid.
Therefore, I am afraid to write because it will confirm that I'm stupid
and don't belong in this program.

Codswallop! Your acceptance into your current program proves you have the potential to think and write well. (Admissions did *not* make a mistake.) Further, difficulty expressing your thoughts in writing does not necessarily mean your thinking about the topic or problem is deficient. But people will evaluate your thinking through your writing. So, you need to develop your thinking about how to write better.

Beliefs about how – even whether – you develop intelligence affect how you approach learning complex skills like writing (Dweck, 2006). Some people consider their intelligence fixed and largely determined by genetics. They've got a knack for writing or they don't. Struggling with their writing means that they aren't cut out for it. Failing proves it. So they give up easily, shying away from challenges and opportunities to improve. They ignore critical feedback because it further confirms that they don't have what it takes (and never will). They feel threatened when others succeed because they do not measure up.

Alternatively, you could cultivate a growth-oriented approach towards intelligence (Dweck, 2006). People with a growth mindset believe that intelligence is malleable and increases with deliberate, sustained effort and adaptive strategy use. Challenges become exciting, struggling equates to learning, setbacks are temporary and surmountable, criticism is constructive, and successful colleagues inspire them. Not surprisingly, students with growth mindsets are more likely to succeed in academic contexts than students with fixed mindsets (Blackwell, Trzeniewski, & Dweck, 2007; Grant & Dweck, 2003).

Take a moment to reflect on your beliefs about intelligence in general and about writing in particular.[1] Do you believe that you can develop your writing skills through deliberate practice and effort? Do setbacks thwart your attempts to write? Do you view writing as an opportunity to learn or as an opportunity to prove that you are smart? Do you seek and use critical feedback to improve your writing? Do you consider others' good writing inspirational and motivational?

If your answers reflect a growth mindset, you have laid some of the groundwork required to develop your writing. If your responses belie a fixed mindset, take heart. You can cultivate a more growth-oriented approach. As a first step, we'll explore how a fixed mindset underlies many misapprehensions about how people become good writers. Then we'll dispel or at least challenge these myths by talking truth. (Even if you are more oriented towards growth, these truths are worth reviewing. They serve as a welcome reality check when the going gets tough.)

Myth: Good Writers Don't Have to Work Hard at Writing; It Comes Naturally to Them[2]

This myth follows directly from the belief that intelligence is a fixed entity. You either possess an innate capability to write well, or you don't. Case closed.

Our cultural conception of the word "struggle" may contribute to this myth. Struggling holds a negative connotation in Western culture; it signals weakness, certain failure, or worse. When you struggle, you may feel that you're an imposter deluding yourself – you are simply not cut out for whatever you're doing (Dweck, 2006).

I invite you to take a step back and look upon struggling as a positive and productive experience. Struggling means that you are being stretched intellectually and emotionally. You may not have achieved your goal yet, but you are well on your way. If things "come easily to you", it is largely because you have sufficiently practiced the skills and organized the knowledge needed to do well, not because of an innate gift.

Truth: Writers Improve their Skills through Deliberate Practice

"Practice makes perfect." This adage is a good start, but it oversimplifies the process of becoming a better writer. How you practice matters. Mindless repetition of rules or drills will not make you a better writer; *deliberate* practice will. Deliberate practice involves typically solitary, goal-directed exercise with the express purpose of improvement (Brown et al., 2014). It is not exactly "fun", either. You identify and chip away at component skills that you've not mastered yet.

Having a fixed mindset does not lend itself to deliberate practice. The very act of practicing involves expending effort. People with fixed mindsets believe that truly smart people should not have to put forth effort because learning comes easily with little training. Dweck (2006), as usual, has the perfect counterargument: "Just because some people can do something with little or no training, it doesn't mean that others can't do it (and sometimes do it even better) with training" (p. 70). Fixed mindsets create a false choice between effort and success. Someone with a fixed mindset who puts forth effort and fails uses that experience to condemn future efforts and reinforce the notion that being good at something comes from inborn talent.

Do not expect that deliberately practicing a skill once or twice will result in a grand transformation. Progress is slow and incremental. Regardless of natural aptitude, it takes about 10 years of deliberate practice to become an expert in cognitively demanding domains, like writing (Ericcson, Krampe, & Tesch-Römer, 1993). To be fair, becoming an expert is different from developing proficiency. But the difference is not qualitative or mystical – it's a question of degree. Deliberately practicing moves you along the continuum towards proficiency and then mastery. Howe (1999) contends that approximately 3000 hours of deliberate practice creates a proficient amateur.

So, writing a quantitative report should not come easily. Writing, as Raymond (1986) notes, is "an unnatural act" that takes time to learn. You have been working towards your 3000 hours for some time and are developing your skills, like most of us. Deliberate practice puts becoming a good writer squarely within your reach and under your direct control. Once you become good, deliberate practice helps you become great.

Myth: Good Writers "Get It Right" The First Time

You may have a friend who can produce a decent paper in a few hours the night before it's due. (And you probably dislike that person.) For those with fixed mindsets, your friend proves the existence of natural-born writers – for the truly smart, first drafts should be as good as final drafts. (They never are.)

Entertain some alternative conclusions for your friend's speed. Perhaps she is a particularly fast typist. Maybe she has mastered grammar, so her sentences sound fluent but are relatively devoid of insight. Perhaps this is not the first time she has written on the topic, so she has developed an elaborate network of concepts that she draws upon to write rapidly.

Becker (2007) surmises that college students can become adept producers of single-draft papers because most college-level assignments are short and bounded by course material that students have been thinking about for most of the semester. Theoretically, a student could hold much of the paper in mind by the time he or she sits down to write and "dump" it. But that strategy won't work with a quantitative research report.

The sheer amount of information contained in your research report demands more than one draft composed in more than one sitting. Your quantitative report is part term paper, technical report, statistical analysis, and critical evaluation all rolled into one. Fully realizing how the components of your report create an integrated whole involves a process of discovery most readily achieved through revision.

Believing that good writers succeed on their first try casts a pall on revision. By that logic, revising is for poor writers. Further, revising takes time and effort, the very things that disgust people with fixed mindsets. Forgoing revision is like vigorously exercising and then skipping your stretch – your muscles stiffen and don't lengthen or strengthen as much. Although your first draft may be passable, you would not obtain full benefit from your effort. Revising helps you truly finish your work and counts as deliberate practice.

Truth: Good Writers Revise, Revise, and Revise Some More

Biographies of beloved writers are riddled with tales of revision. Ernest Hemingway is rumored to have rewritten the final page of *A Farewell to Arms* over 30 times. F. Scott Fitzgerald marked out page upon page of handwritten text in early drafts of *The Great Gatsby*. These authors were not satisfied with their first, second, or even third drafts. You shouldn't be, either.

If you commit to produce multiple drafts, you should develop a realistic impression of what a first draft should accomplish. You write a first draft to learn about what you want to say and how you want to say it (Flower, 1979; McCloskey, 2000; Zinsser, 1988). First drafts are supposed to be hot messes. (I will happily send you the first draft of this chapter as proof.) Consider an artist making preliminary sketches of a larger work. Do you think Michelangelo's frescos in the Sistine Chapel were first drafts? Early drafts enable you to play with ideas, forms, and modes of expression. Some things work; others don't. If you approach your quantitative report knowing that the first draft is not the final draft, you feel free to explore and take risks (Becker, 2007).

After you put your first draft away for a day or two, look at it again with fresh, critical eyes. Subsequent drafts offer the opportunity to refine expression and explore connections. Ideas that seemed crystal clear before now confuse you. Once elegant sounding sentences clunkily clang. No matter how experienced a writer you become, you will continue to marvel at how far you progress from a first draft.

Myth: Good Writers Wait for Inspiration to Hit Before Starting to Write

Ah, the muse. When Homer invoked Calliope to inspire the *Odyssey* and the *Illiad*, he unwittingly encouraged people with fixed mindsets to chase rather than command their muse. Writing only while inspired gives the false impression that writing should feel effortless. Once inspiration hits, ideas spring forth rapidly and easily. Csikszentmihalyi (1996) calls this feeling of total immersion "flow". And it feels *amazing*. You are "in the zone" or "in the pocket" and produce your "best, most efficient, and most satisfying writing" (Flower & Hayes, 1977, p. 451).

But waiting for inspiration or flow is problematic for several reasons. First, wait too long and you flirt with disaster. (This is better known as procrastination.) Second, many of the challenges writers face require focused problem-solving strategies, not inspiration (Flower & Hayes, 1977). Third, inspiration makes writers feel productive, but it could be an illusion brought on by massed practice (Brown et al., 2014). In a single inspired session you go from nothing to something, which feels like a big difference. Multiple more labored sessions feel as if you are not progressing as rapidly towards your goals. But you would be pleasantly surprised if you tracked your progress (Silvia, 2007).

Call it a muse, inspiration, flow, or procrastination – they can all lead to the same self-defeating end: writing will get done hastily or not at all. The author E. B. White said in an interview, "A writer who waits for ideal conditions under which to work will die without putting a word on paper."

Truth: Good Writers Schedule their Writing Time and Stick to their Schedule

The best writers, like anyone else at the top of their field, are disciplined. They deliberately practice even when they don't feel particularly inspired (Keyes, 2003; Silvia, 2007). To become disciplined, you need to do three things: schedule your writing time, make clear goals for each writing session, and track your progress.

You do not need large chunks of time to make steady progress on writing your report. Try to schedule 5 hours a week, preferably 1 hour per day over 5 days. If you stick to this schedule, you will have devoted about 75 hours over a 15-week semester. Would you rather those hours be spread out over 15 weeks? Or crammed into 2? Or 1?!?

Set concrete, actionable goals (e.g., write 100 words, draft the first two paragraphs of your report). Goals do not necessarily involve putting words on the page (Silvia, 2007). You could read and take notes on an article, outline a section, perform analyses, make figures and tables – anything that gets you closer to completing your report. That said, I would devote at least 2 sessions a week to actual writing. Otherwise, you can end up putting off writing for too long.

Given that you are conducting quantitative research, you know a thing or two about collecting data. So you know how to collect data measuring your own writing progress. Choose meaningful metrics. The most important one is simply whether you stuck to your writing schedule. You will have good sessions and grim sessions, but you can still check the win column when you're done. You could also track word count or page count. Running up counts is easier when you are drafting. When you are revising, the goal is to *decrease* word and page counts because you are refining your thinking and tightening your prose.

This discipline reaps rewards. First, writing regularly increases insight, where the pieces of an intractable puzzle suddenly fit. Although insight feels like a bolt from the blue, it arises from your brain mulling over a problem outside your conscious awareness (Metcalfe & Weibe, 1987). Insight arrives only after the ideas or details have had time to incubate (Flower & Hayes, 1977). Adhering to your writing schedule builds incubation into your routine.

Second, adhering to a schedule means that you no longer passively await your muse or "flow"; you create conditions that promote it (Csikszentmihalyi, 1996). For example, minimizing distractions (i.e., turning off your phone, social media, etc.) allows you to devote your full attention to your task. Adjusting the amount of challenge you experience also helps. When your skill level exceeds the task, you get bored. When tasks are beyond your skill level, you get frustrated. So, the trick is to set goals that ratchet up the challenge as you are building the skill. Realistically, do not expect to get into flow during every writing session. No matter your skill level, checking your references for accuracy is a yawner.

Third, writing habitually reduces your anxiety about writing a quantitative research report. You are solving a complex, multifaceted problem. Routinely chipping away at larger goals by focusing on smaller ones ensures that you will make steady progress.

Sticking to your schedule is tough, but sometimes the bigger hurdle is establishing the schedule in the first place. You have to be committed to the goal, decide how much time you are willing to devote, and identify and remove barriers. Let me share a personal example. I had convinced myself that my life simply would not tolerate regular exercise. I couldn't go to the gym or leave my house for extended periods of time because of familial responsibilities. So my first challenge was figuring out duration and a time of day I could stick with. I decided on 30 minutes a day, 5 days a week before the kids woke up. The second barrier was figuring out how to exercise in my home. I found a series of DVDs that fit my time constraints and kept me motivated. At first progress was slow. But in a little over a year, I am enjoying the benefits of being in good physical condition. I am now applying the same lessons to my writing. (Sometimes we come late to the party, but at least we show up.)

Myth: Good Writers Sound Smart

People with fixed mindsets emphasize performance; writing is a way to perform and express intelligence. In the hands of fixed-mindset drivers, writing becomes a vehicle to prove intellectual elitism. Many authors of scholarly sources certainly sound intelligent, but at what cost? Prose becomes overblown with 5-dollar words, complicated constructions, and information about anything that is remotely related to the problem at hand.

Ironically, students with fixed mindsets do not respond well when reading smart-sounding, but ultimately unintelligible prose:

> When I read something and I don't know immediately what it means, I always give the author the benefit of the doubt. I assume this is a smart person and the problem with my not understanding the ideas is that I'm not smart… I always assume that it is my inability to understand or that there is something more going on than I'm capable of understanding… I assume if it got into [a prestigious journal], for example, chances are it's good and it's important and if I don't understand it that's my problem since the journal has already legitimated it. (Becker, 2007, p. 29)

Hence the vicious cycle: perceptions of inferiority drive emerging researchers to prove themselves by emulating a style that avails knowledge to an elite few. It's time to break the cycle.

Truth: Good Writers Work to Make their Prose Accessible and Engaging

Writing that most people do not understand has limited utility. I do not advocate oversimplifying or avoiding complexities. However, you must keep readers on board. You can engage readers without sacrificing intellectual rigor by accepting that "good writing is good teaching" (Bem, 2004, p. 4).

How do the best teachers engage their students? Bain (2004) offers some keen suggestions, which I will extend to writing your quantitative research report. Good teachers know their discipline; good writers know their topic and their data well. Sharing this knowledge does not involve cataloging information. Rather, writers take a reader-centered approach, tailoring material to readers' needs. Good writers constantly evaluate their writing from the reader's perspective, assessing what readers currently know and what they might need to know before encountering a forthcoming point.

Good teachers have high standards for their students and create environments in which students can reach these expectations (Bain, 2004). Similarly, good writers should challenge readers to up their game. You want your reader to learn something new and useful, or view an important problem from a different perspective. However, you must create conditions within your writing that enable readers to achieve this goal.

Effective teachers infuse lessons with humor and novelty to keep learners engaged. Keeping your readers engaged is not so different from keeping readers entertained. McCloskey (2000) argues:

> Most academic prose, from both students and faculty, could use more humor. There is nothing unscientific about self-deprecating jokes about the sample size, and nothing unscholarly in dry wit about the failings of intellectual proponents. (p. 43)

Humor, more than any other rhetorical device, requires bravery. Be prepared for your attempts to tank every now and again, and be proud that you attempted to enliven the conversation.

Novelty captures – or recaptures – readers' interest. You can achieve novelty by avoiding the "boilerplate" that plagues academic prose (McCloskey, 2000). Boilerplate offerings include the predictable, mundane, and soulless. Describing every source you read, skimmed, or threw a parting glance towards qualifies as academic boilerplate. Professors identify padding the way hawks spot mice. (It doesn't end well for the mouse.) McCloskey (2000) also warns writers against using the "roadmap" paragraph to introduce sections of your report. She is convinced that the well-meaning high school English teacher who coined "Tell the reader what you are going to say. Say it. Say that you've said it," is burning in Hell.

Good writers engage readers without sacrificing nuance or critical thinking. Like good teachers, good writers breathe life into their report.[3] The result? Everyone learns.

Myth: Good Writers Do Not Share their Writing with Others

People with a fixed mindset have a dysfunctional relationship with feedback. They may not seek feedback at all because smart people should not have to rely on others to produce excellent work. Alternatively, people might seek feedback from sources that provide unconditional affirmation (Honey, you've always been such a good writer!"). And they regularly avoid or ignore critical feedback because it threatens their self-concept. If you believe that your intelligence manifests in your writing, feedback becomes a referendum on your intelligence (Stone & Heen, 2014).

Hearing that your writing doesn't make the grade can trigger defensive thoughts (Stone & Heen, 2014). Negative feedback indicts your identity (e.g., "I screw everything up"), and may call you to question its truth (e.g., "They're just wrong; they clearly didn't understand what I was trying to say."). You also might question your relationship with the person delivering the feedback (e.g., "She's out to get me. She plays favorites.").

None of these thoughts will make you a better writer. Learning how to effectively seek and process critical feedback will.

Truth: Good Writers Actively Seek and Process Feedback to Improve their Writing

Feedback serves at least two important purposes. First, receiving feedback from a master teacher or coach can jumpstart learning (Ericcson et al., 1993). When people are developing skill through deliberate practice, they frequently plateau (Brown et al., 2014). Feedback helps learners focus their attention and practice more effectively.

Second, feedback lets you know whether you are hitting your mark with your audience. You might write with your audience in mind, but your imagined audience is not the same as the real thing. For example, the writers and cast members of *Saturday Night Live* have a weekly ritual testing skits during Wednesday writers' meetings and then again at a dress rehearsal hours before the live show on Saturday. Sometimes a skit can destroy on Wednesday, but die at dress because the writers have constructed the skit for other comedy writers, not for the audience.[4]

As a student, you can fortunately turn to many people for feedback. Establish a network. Your professor is a logical choice, assuming that she is amenable to reviewing your drafts. (A word to the wise: Ask for feedback *in person*. E-mailing your professor with the subject line "Can u just look this over for me?" may not be the best approach.) Teaching assistants or peer tutors can serve as sounding boards or informal reviewers. Your classmates are also excellent candidates because they share the experience of writing a quantitative research report. Consider forming a writing group where you review each other's drafts. Because delivering criticism can be just as difficult as receiving it, establish ground rules that invite constructive criticism as well as affirmation.

Criticism can be hard to hear, but there are some strategies you can use to increase the likelihood that you benefit from the feedback. First, think of the feedback less as an evaluation of your performance and more as coaching (Stone & Heen, 2014). People providing feedback hope that their comments can help you improve; they do not intend to cut you down. Second, when you receive particularly negative feedback, focus on your response to that feedback (Stone & Heen, 2014). Grade yourself. If you can tell yourself that you may have earned a C on the paper, but you handled it like an A, you are more likely to succeed the next time. You are not deluding yourself; you are cultivating the grit and optimism that underlie success (Duckworth, Peterson, Matthews, & Kelly, 2007; Seligman, 2006).

THE RULES

You learn the rules so you can have fun (McCloskey, 2000). You may associate the rules of writing with grammar, that interminable assault of niggly traps whose sole purpose is to make your life miserable. Proper grammar is important; without it, you cannot communicate clearly. But we will not review grammatical rules here.[5] (Did I just hear a sigh of relief?) Rather, we will discuss broader principles that underlie writing a strong quantitative report.

Rule #1: Learn the Major Sections of the Report with Your Bare Hands

Quantitative research reports impose an overarching structure consisting of several major sections. Appreciating the organization of a research report makes it much easier to decide what you want to do with your knowledge (Flower & Hayes, 1977). Use this blueprint to plan your writing and break complex goals into more manageable ones.

Just as there is more than One Right Way to express ideas, there is more than One Right Way to organize the major sections of the research report. The most common organization across the social and behavioral sciences is like a human hand, or what I call "The Humanoid" (see Figure 3.1).

We'll address the detailed components that comprise each "digit" throughout the rest of this book. For now, we'll concern ourselves with describing the broad function of each section. The Introduction acquaints readers with your research question and convinces them why they should care about your research. The Literature Review educates readers about what scholars currently know about your research question and leads to your predictions. The Method details how you obtained your data, including who or what you sampled. The Results (or Analysis) section presents your findings. The Discussion contextualizes your findings and identifies limitations, areas of future study, and broader implications of your work.

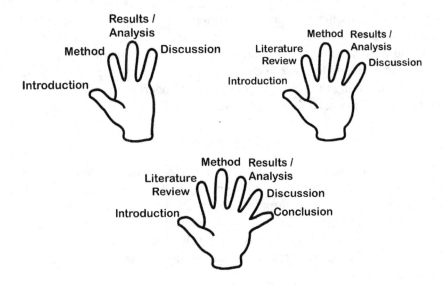

Figure 3.1. The "bare hand" approach to organizing the quantitative research report, including the "The Simpson 4", "The Humanoid 5", and "The Count Rugen 6"

Sometimes you will see the overall organization extended to six digits. (Think Count Rugen in *The Princess Bride*.) The additional phalange is the Conclusion, which appears after the Discussion (see Figure 3.1). The Conclusion serves to highlight what is usually the final paragraph in the Discussion of the 5-digit approach: to state in a nutshell what you examined, why you studied it, what you found, what it means, and why someone should care.

The streamlined, 4-digit approach (or, *The Simpsons*) is typical in Psychological Science. The Introduction, taking its cue from the Borg, assimilates the Literature Review (see Figure 3.1).[6]

Now that you have a sense of a report's general organization, consider how you might approach composing the digits. When I write a research report, I draw upon a literary analogy. To me, a research report is a novel: you set the scene, introduce characters, and establish plot points; insert rising action; reach the climax; and fall back while wrapping up loose ends and leaving your reader with something to think about. Your Introduction and Literature Review orient readers and introduce important characters and plot points. Your Method gets things moving. Your Results and Analysis are the answers to your questions (finally!). Your Discussion and Conclusion sum up everything and address lingering concerns.

My literary analogy is not the only approach: Mark Edwards (2012), a sociologist, imagines himself as a prosecuting attorney presenting a case. He presents opening arguments in the Introduction, introduces relevant facts in the Literature Review, explains how he obtained evidence in the Method, lays out the evidence in the Results, and delivers closing arguments in the Discussion/Conclusion.

Whatever your analogy, you are about to embark on an exciting journey writing your report. When you complete this adventure, perhaps you will develop your own analogy. I'd love to hear about it.

Rule #2: Write to Learn. Then Write to Teach

Watch a 3-year-old play by herself and you will observe something fascinating: she'll start a conversation… with herself. She talks to express her thoughts as they are happening in real time with no goal of communicating her ideas to anyone in particular. Eavesdropping on this private monologue yields amusement and more than a bit of confusion. She seems to know exactly what she is talking about, but we observers are lost. It's as if she's talking in code and making connections that make perfect sense to her but we can't follow. Cognitive developmental psychologists have called this phenomenon "egocentric speech" (Piaget, 1926) or "inner speech" (Vygotsky, 1962).

Flower (1979) contends that egocentric or inner speech manifests as "writer-based prose" in adulthood. It is a record of your thought process, typically recorded in narrative form and containing terms that hold rich meaning for you (but not your reader). Writer-based prose is, then, a form of goal-directed play (Flower & Hayes, 1977). It is a wonderful way to learn about what you think at a given time. Thoughts are ephemeral and often elusive – writing thoughts down gives them shape, which makes them easier to manipulate and hone.

You can enter into writer-based prose using many strategies (Flower & Hayes, 1977). First, you can brainstorm ideas without censoring yourself. Let the ideas flow. Remember that you are writing to learn at this stage – don't worry whether your notions are half-baked or your language is unpolished. Turn off the editor and go. Second, you can take a cue from the 3-year-old and stage a conversation. (Depending on your location, you may want to make this an internal dialogue.) Unlike the preschooler, however, you're conversing with your intended audience. What would your audience ask you? How would you respond? Third, try an analogy. Connecting ideas through analogical reasoning opens up a world of additional concepts to play with. (You may have noticed that I use analogy a fair bit.)

41

"Writing to learn" (Becker, 2007; McCloskey, 2000; Zinsser, 2001) reveals your current level of understanding. Thinking about writing in this manner frees you from requiring all the information to be clear in your mind before committing it to the page (Flower, 1979); it also commits you to revision. Once you have written to learn about what you think, you set about teaching it to your audience.

Rule #3: Report, Support, Do Not Distort

You and your reader share a mutual end: to understand what you asked, why you asked it, what you did, what you found, and what your findings mean. To this end, you need to report information accurately, support claims with credible evidence and/or theory, and convey information with fidelity.

Report information accurately. Accurately communicating information marks you as a developing professional – someone who can be trusted to find, generate, and share information responsibly. Within your report, you will summarize scholarly literature relevant to your research question and state your findings. To report information accurately, you must first understand it.

Emerging researchers can be intimidated by scholarly literature. A fair amount of scholarly literature – let's face it – has been not written with accessibility as its top priority. Reread sections that do not make sense on the first pass (this will happen a lot). Jot down unfamiliar jargon and specific questions and consult your academic network... the one you established to provide feedback on your work. Be optimistic – the literature becomes easier to read the more familiar you become with the topic and with the structure of academic writing.

Grasping your statistical analysis and your findings might concern you more than understanding the literature. Maintain focus on your research question(s). Remember, statistical analysis is a tool to answer questions, not to bring on a migraine. Clarify questions about the execution of your analysis or the content of your findings with your network.

Once you have developed a clear understanding of the literature and your findings, accessed your support network, and drafted your sections, it's time to fact-check. Go back to the literature and carefully evaluate your characterization of the information. Return to your data analysis and review your conclusions. Confirm that you have reported all statistical values accurately. It is a tedious process, but the alternative (i.e., inaccurately reporting literature or findings) is far less attractive.

Support your claims. "Half of the marriages in the US end in divorce." Everyone knows that, right? It's not so simple. Depending on how you measure divorce, the divorce rate has never reached 50% (more like 41%; Krieder, 2005). And more recent trends reveal a notable decline in divorce rate, particularly for well-educated women since the late 1970s (Martin, n.d.). Yet, the assertion is so ubiquitous we rarely question it. Your lesson: substantiate empirical or theoretical claims with a credible source.

What sources are considered credible? You may feel so personally connected to your research question that you want to use your own experience or intuition to justify predictions or conclusions. Personal connections can fuel the questions you ask and help motivate you to persist, but they are not scientifically credible. Your personal experiences may not represent the population and are colored by your idiosyncratic perceptions.

Favor scholarly sources, such as peer-reviewed journal articles, books, and chapters in edited books. Unpublished manuscripts and dissertations may be acceptable, but they have not been peer-reviewed and should not comprise the bulk of your scholarly support.

The popular press (e.g., *Time, The Wall Street Journal*, the *Economist*) could prove useful in limited circumstances. For example, a quantitative report examining potential explanations of school violence might begin: "After the Columbine massacre in Littleton, Colorado, the cover of *Newsweek* posed a single question: 'Why?' (Newsweek, 1999)." So, you could use the popular press to hook your reader and convey that your topic directly relates to a real-world problem. However, you would not use popular sources as part of your literature review or to rationalize your predictions.

Supporting your claims will convince others that you are a serious emerging researcher, but over-citing can backfire. For example, you do not need to reference statements of historical fact (e.g., The Declaration of Independence was signed on July 4, 1776) or definitive truth (e.g., Mammals have hair or fur). Further, once you've cited a source within a paragraph, you do not need to cite it again unless you are using it in a different context. Let's say you are describing an empirical study in three sequential sentences. Cite the author(s) in the first sentence only. Some conscientious students cite nearly every sentence within a literature review, creating information overload.

Convey information ethically. In addition to accurately relaying information and sufficiently substantiating claims, you must convey information ethically. The scientific enterprise relies upon integrity to move our understanding of the human condition forward. When you act unethically, you erode people's confidence in you and in science. As such, you must give proper credit to others' work, convey information in your own words, and hold your data inviolate.

Plagiarism involves improperly crediting someone's work. Imagine that you have completed your quantitative project after much blood, sweat, and tears. You're watching the campus news and up pops your professor who happens to be describing your project. How exciting! And she never mentions your name. (Really?!?) Always give credit where credit is due.

Referencing a source implies that you have carefully evaluated it. The literature reviews of the primary sources you read will likely include other works that look relevant for your research project. To cite these sources, you must locate them and read them yourself. In so doing you confirm that the source is indeed relevant and you ensure that you represent the work accurately, rather than take someone else's word for it (even if the source should count as credible). In the rare event that you cannot locate the primary source, you can cite the secondary source. (You can learn more about referencing sources in Chapter 8.)

It's not enough to simply reference your sources. Expressing an author's words in a slightly different format (i.e., changing a word here and there) is also plagiarism because you are presenting that author's voice largely as your own. Here's a rule of thumb: If four or more consecutive words are identical to the source, you are at risk for plagiarizing.

Some emerging researchers try to sidestep plagiarism by immaculately transcribing and citing multiple direct quotes. Although direct quotes can be valuable when defining a construct or operationalizing a variable, use them judiciously. Including too many quotations introduces a problem: A bunch of unconnected, incoherent ideas. The goal is to paraphrase, or to state something in your own words (and then properly cite the authors).

If you find yourself thinking, "I can't paraphrase because I could never express this idea as well as the original author did," you're mistaken. Remember that everyone writes with a specific goal in mind. You are writing in a different context, one with a specific purpose known only by you. Thus, you should present the information in a way that furthers *your* purpose and tells *your* story. (To be clear, tailoring your writing does NOT mean reporting information inaccurately or omitting crucial information because you think it strengthens your argument.)

How do you paraphrase effectively? Try this: Read the information that you want to write about. Recite (out loud, if possible) the most important information from the source and how you could use the information in your paper (e.g., theory, major construct of interest, etc.). Put the source out of sight. Choose a 3-digit number (e.g., 836) and start counting backwards by 3s (or 4s, 6s, or 7s if you want to mix it up) for at least 30 seconds. Counting backwards should dislodge verbatim traces (i.e., exact wording) that might linger in your short-term memory. What remains is the gist, or general idea of the information, which you then express in your own words.

In addition to conveying others' work ethically, you must collect and present your data ethically. There are far too many reports of scientists bowing to pressure and fabricating or altering data. Few examples are more powerful than the scandal surrounding the MMR (Measles, Mumps, Rubella) vaccine and autism (e.g., Dominus, 2011). In 1998, Dr. Andrew Wakefield (and others) published a report claiming that the MMR vaccine was linked to the appearance of autism-like behaviors in 12 young children. This finding received a great deal of media attention and prompted thousands of parents to avoid vaccinating their toddlers. However, multiple studies (and hundreds of thousands of dollars) could not replicate Wakefield's findings. A British investigative journalist, Brian Deer, claimed that Wakefield misrepresented the symptom timeline of most, if not all his participants. Coupled with other questionable behavior (e.g., taking blood samples from children at his son's birthday party because he needed data from non-symptomatic controls, and accepting money for research from lawyers attempting to sue MMR vaccine makers), Great Britain's General Medical Council banned Wakefield from practicing medicine. Although Wakefield experienced serious personal repercussions, a far more pressing problem is an outbreak of measles in young adolescents, some of whose parents refused to vaccinate their children for fear of autism ("Aftermath of an Unfounded Vaccine Scare", 2013).

You can feel frustrated and disheartened when your results do not pan out the way you had hoped. But your data are your data. Come by them ethically and report them ethically. Distorting or fabricating your results can have disastrous consequences that extend beyond your personal sphere of influence.

Rule #4: Collect and Connect the Dots

In works of fiction, you may have encountered stream-of-consciousness prose, as in J.D. Salinger's *Catcher in the Rye*. You are transported into Holden Caufield's mind and the way he sees the world around him. But you are left wondering whether he actually experienced certain events. Were they dreams or fantasies? Fiction, particularly literary fiction, is rife with opportunity to make inferences – that is how readers become engaged in the plot and in the development of the characters. But in expository works (i.e., quantitative research) explicit connections and well-justified conclusions reign supreme.

National Public Radio commends its journalists for "collecting and connecting the dots" for their listeners. That's what you need to do for your readers. It's not enough to convey relevant details accurately and ethically; you need to explicitly convey how information connects within and across sections of your report. The very best expository writers make us feel as if we are strolling through their extremely logical brain. (And we remind ourselves that these wonderful writers' first drafts were not nearly so orderly or accessible!)

Connecting the dots requires a transition from writer- to reader-based prose (Flower, 1979). Writer-based prose reveals a writer's unfolding process of discovery – like listening to people describe their dreams:

> I began thinking about why people would argue against amnesty for illegal immigrants. Could it be that they are afraid of immigrants collecting on entitlements that are un- or underfunded? Are they concerned that illegal immigrants would take their jobs because they would be willing to work for less?

You can see that the author is identifying some interesting ideas here (e.g., entitlements, competition for jobs). But the structure makes it difficult for readers to follow. The writer overuses pronouns (e.g., they) and the reader is not sure whether the author means illegal immigrants or US citizens who oppose amnesty for illegal immigrants. The good news is that the kernels of a solid argument emerge from writer-based prose. You can return to these ideas and rework them, keeping readers' needs squarely in mind.

Writer-based prose is rife with "code words" that hold rich meaning for the writer, and virtually none for the reader. Consider the following sentence:

> Women have recently become empowered to become individuals and achieve success in life.

This sentence may make perfect sense to the writer. Readers, however, are left wondering how recent is "recent", what it means to "become an individual", and how "success" is defined in this context. Good news! You can readily address these questions in revision.

How can you tell whether you are conveying your thoughts explicitly enough? Ask someone to read your work and explain it back to you. If she does not clearly specify the connections between concepts, you have likely jumped from Point A to Point C without realizing you glossed over Point B. If she emphasizes relatively unimportant points, you have missed your mark. Then buy her coffee or a snack – providing feedback is not easy, and she has helped you improve your work.

You could also try reading your prose aloud, firmly and deliberately (Flower & Hayes, 1977; McCloskey, 2000). Doing so will short-circuit the internal editor that visually skims over clunky constructions and subconsciously scans for points you intended to emphasize. As you read, mark places where you trip over words or slow down; that's your brain working harder to process the material (Ferreira, 1991). You can also record yourself reading your work and then listen to it without following your "script". Hearing how you intone your prose reveals what your reader will likely emphasize.

Rule #5: Write for Your Audience (Which is categorically not Wikipedia)

Don't get caught writing your quantitative report for Wikipedia. You go to Wikipedia to obtain detailed, exhaustive, and exhausting information: What is this concept? Who did this? How many supermodels has Leonardo DiCaprio dated? You skim until you find the information you're looking for and off you go.

If not Wikipedia users, whom are you writing for? "A learned, highly trained community of scholars," you say? Forget that. Take Daryl Bem's (2004) advice and make your writing accessible to the widest audience possible.

Write for interested, but relatively inexperienced readers in your field— your classmates. They have some introductory level of knowledge about your discipline, so don't concern yourself with defining basic methodological or statistical terms such as "validity" or "standard deviation". However, assume that your classmates have little to no knowledge about the constructs you are studying. At the end of the day, you want your classmates to glean the overarching purpose of your study, what you found (in broad strokes), and why they should care about it.

Thus far we have discussed how you tailor content for your audience, but we haven't spoken about tone. Throughout this book, my tone has been mostly conversational and playful. I use certain rhetorical devices to capture interest and keep you engaged, yes? I vary punctuation… I adore parenthetical commentary (cheeky though it may be). And, humor, well—

how could I successfully write a book about quantitative research without humor?

McCloskey (2000) contends that an author's tone and clarity "depends on choosing and then keeping an appropriate implied author, the character you pretend to be while you're writing" (p. 39). Currently, I'm performing the role of The Hip-But-Awkward-Overinvested-Teutonism-Loving-Professor (somewhat successfully, I hope). In your writing, you should aspire to portray The Emerging Researcher.

Indulge me while I sketch my conception of The Emerging Researcher. She respects but does not revere other researchers' work. She generates knowledge to better understand humankind. She participates in the enterprise of scientific inquiry with integrity and fidelity. Serious and intrepid, she embraces her project with a sense of wonder and discovery. She persists through setbacks and solves problems using adaptive strategies. She understands that the goal of writing a research report is not to document what she knows but to teach her readers something worthwhile.

Now go win an Academy Award.

Rule #6: Seek Ye the 3 C's – Clear, Concise, Coherent

To make your work accessible to a wide audience, you need to communicate clearly, concisely, and coherently (Flower, 1993). Your ideas may be brilliant and your findings compelling, but they will fall flat without clear, concise, and coherent expression. Focusing on these three goals helps you shift from writer-based to reader-based prose.

Clear. You achieve clarity when your audience understands what you intended to convey. To improve clarity, identify code words and unpack them. Be explicit.

Not as clear as it could be: The Pew Research Center, who conducted a study in 2011, contends that young adults between the ages of 18 to 24 are enrolling in college in record numbers. They go on to note that student debt has increased exponentially.

Clearer: According to the Pew Research Center (2011), the percentage of 18- to 24-year-olds enrolled in college has increased approximately 70% since the 1960s. However, student debt has more than tripled since the 1980s, exceeding $20,000 on average.

Concise. Concise writing renders every word essential – no fluff, no redundancy, just powerful prose. Strategies to increase conciseness include:

- Destroying "filler". Is every article (e.g., *the, a*) required? Can you change singular nouns to plural? Have you included tautologies (e.g., *two twins, hot lava*)? Are all qualifiers (e.g., *I think that...* or *I read that*) necessary? Are all modifiers (e.g., *very, interestingly*) warranted? Have you overused the construction "There is..."?
- Condensing many words into fewer words. Prepositional phrases are prime candidates: "The dog that belonged to my father during his childhood" can be reduced to "My father's childhood dog".
- Identifying signals of redundancy (e.g., *As I said earlier...*) and removing or reorganizing information accordingly.
- Writing with active verbs and in active voice. Traditional academic writing notoriously obscures agents of action (Becker, 2007). I could have written the previous sentence as: "Agents of action are notoriously obscured by traditional academic writing." (Blech.)

Consider the following prose and its subsequent revision. Try to identify which strategies I used to improve conciseness.

> *Not concise*: "I think that the series *Song of Ice and Fire* by George R. R. Martin is an epic tale of magnificent scale. There are no fewer than 30 major characters, and the story is periodically told from each character's point of view." (42 words)

> *More concise*: "George R. R. Martin's *Song of Ice and Fire* unfolds on an epic scale. No fewer than 30 characters narrate the story from their unique viewpoint." (26 words – Booyah!)

Coherent. Coherent writing organizes and connects ideas within a logical framework, gently shepherding your readers across intellectual pastures. It's tough work. Fashioning clarity and conciseness occurs *within* sentences; forging coherence occurs *between* sentences, paragraphs, and sections. According to Flower (1993), effective writers work towards achieving coherence locally (i.e., between sentences) and globally (i.e., between paragraphs).

You achieve local coherence by linking ideas between sentences. *Conjunctive adverbs* or *adverbial phrases* (a.k.a. *transitions* or *linking words*) telegraph how sentences are related, contrastive, illustrative, or conclusive. To signal readers that information will support an initial claim, begin a sentence with "In addition" or "Further". To denote a contrastive perspective or conflicting evidence, use "By contrast", "Alternatively", "However", "Whereas", or "On the other hand". "For example" illustrates a concept. To move towards a conclusion, use "Thus", "Consequently", or "Therefore".

A word of caution: Treat transitions like caffeine. Judicious use can get you over the occasional hump. Overuse creates tolerance, and you rely on them just to function. Linking words quickly become tedious and readers may resent your "pushing them around" (McCloskey, 2000).

Repetition can remedy overreliance on transitions and supply built-in coherence (McCloskey, 2000). Examine the preceding paragraph – the theme is to exercise care in using transitions. The unifying thread throughout the paragraph is the concept of "transition", although it is expressed differently in each sentence. Sometimes I use the pronoun "them"; in another sentence I use the synonym "linking word" that I introduced in a previous paragraph. And I have shamelessly exploited repetition in this paragraph.

Local coherence begins with a strong topic sentence to introduce the goal or theme of the paragraph (e.g., to present the problem under study, to establish theoretical underpinnings of a phenomenon, etc.). Subsequent sentences advance the theme. Sentences that do not align with the theme should be flagged for relocation or outright omission. In the language of psychology, a topic sentence establishes a schema or a framework that makes supporting details much easier to comprehend. Read the following paragraph:

> The procedure is actually quite simple. First you arrange things into different groups. Of course, one pile may be sufficient depending on how much there is to do. If you have to go somewhere else due to lack of facilities that is the next step, otherwise you are pretty well set. It is important not to overdo things. That is, it is better to do too few things at once than too many. (adapted from Bransford & Johnson, 1972, p. 722)

Read it again after inserting this topic sentence: "Doing laundry doesn't have to be stressful." A strong topic sentence makes all the difference. Topic sentences claim alpha status within the hierarchy of a paragraph; all subsequent sentences are subordinate.

Writers also attempt to establish a hierarchical structure between paragraphs. Here, too, topic sentences play a pivotal role: they orient readers to from one major idea or claim to the next, forming the bedrock of global coherence. A quantitative report could begin: "Obesity has reached epidemic proportions in the United States and has become a critical public health issue." Your readers expect you describe this epidemic (e.g., How has the rate of obesity changed over the past 40 years?) and explain how obesity has impacted public health (e.g., Has the incidence of weight-related diseases such as Type II diabetes changed?). The next paragraph might start, "Multiple societal forces have exacerbated the rise of adult obesity." Now readers anticipate these forces and you would devote subsequent paragraphs to identifying the forces you investigated in your study.

Writers have developed many strategies to achieve global coherence. At some point during your education, you've likely been compelled to create an outline. Although outlines certainly help writers organize their thoughts and establish structure, writing with an outline may encourage you to "fill in the details", inadvertently encouraging you to document for yourself rather than teach your reader.

Alternatively, you could impose structure after you've begun to generate ideas. Flower and Hayes (1977) suggest "treeing" your ideas – that is, imposing a hierarchical structure on idea fragments. In so doing, you form a graphic representation of how your thoughts interconnect and you can identify holes or gaps in your thinking. For example, let's say that you have investigated whether "sounding gay" predicts success in the workplace. Your idea fragments include:

• Gay men typically produce rising intonation at the end of sentences.
• Gay men are perceived as less competent than heterosexual men.
• Gay men emphasize sibilants (e.g., "s") in their speech
• Gay men have a stereotypical speech pattern.
• Gay men's speech has been popularized and stereotyped in media.
• Gay men make less money on average than heterosexual men.

Figure 3.2 illustrates how your tree might look.

By treeing your ideas, you realize that your fragment regarding gay men's speech being popularized in media doesn't fit here in the existing structure. So, you need to build a new branch of the tree or omit it. Treeing fragments can also lead to new questions: Are there other stereotypical features of gay men's speech, such as higher pitch or vocal fry (i.e., a low, growling sound)? Why would speech production be related to workplace success? Is "sounding gay" perceived as effeminate? Do women who sound more effeminate undermine their workplace success?

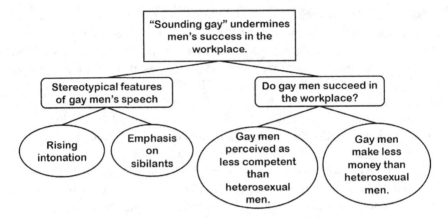

Figure 3.2. How to "tree" ideas to establish global coherence

Upon finishing your draft, you might not be convinced that your ideas globally cohere. Read your topic sentences sequentially.[7] If they form a coherent summary of that section, you have constructed strong global coherence.

Whatever your strategy, remember *Project Runway* and religiously invoke Tim Gunn's catchphrase: "Make it work". That said, do not be afraid to scrap an organizational structure that simply does not work. Reframing the building may be a better option than retrofitting an ultimately unworkable structure. Expert writers recognize when to raze and rebuild (Flower, 1993).

Rule #7 – Language!

Mark Twain notably quipped, "The difference between the right word and the almost right word is the difference between lightning and a lightning bug." Words pack a punch, and we can be tempted to throw knockouts because they forcefully convey our ideas. However, nudges can be just as or more effective.

Choose your words felicitously and cautiously, especially when discussing causal relationships between variables. You've memorized the adage, "Correlation does not imply causation." However, you may not be clear about the conditions under which you can make a causal claim. To establish a casual claim, a relationship must meet three criteria (Morling, 2015). First, variables must covary (i.e., a reliable relationship must exist). Second, one variable must clearly precede another (i.e., the cause must precede the effect). Third, alternative explanations must be addressed and minimized.

In behavioral sciences, experiments involving a true manipulation and exercising reasonably rigorous control meet all three criteria. Some longitudinal designs (i.e., testing the same individuals at multiple time periods) also point towards a causal conclusion because temporal precedence can be clearly established. Certain advanced statistical techniques can *suggest* the direction of a causal relationship when temporal precedence is murky. Becker (2007) contends that emerging researchers shy away from making causal claims because they are too timid to play intellectual hardball. You're not wimping out if your research design or analysis cannot support a causal conclusion.

Selecting the appropriate word requires knowing its definition. (Thank you, Professor Obvious.) Still, certain words are pathologically misused. Some books on writing devote entire chapters to usage errors (e.g., Edwards, 2012; Strunk & White, 2005), and disciplinary formatting guides (e.g., APA, 2012; ASA, 2010) document these errors with impressive zeal. For our purposes, Table 3.1 will suffice.

Table 3.1. Common misusages

Misusage	Description
Affect vs. effect	The words "affect" and "effect" can be used as nouns as well as verbs. "Affect" as a verb means to change something (e.g., Sitting in a hot room *affected* how aggressively participants acted.). Conversely, "effect" as a noun conveys the result of some change (e.g., I investigated the effect of "trickle-down economics" on the rural poor).
Since vs. because	"Since" and "because" are not synonyms. "Since" refers to the passage of time (e.g., "Since the women's liberation movement of the 1960s and 70s, feminist literature has become a cultural mainstay.") "Because" conveys causality. Despite your middle-school English teacher's dogged insistence, you can use "because" at the beginning of a complete sentence (e.g., "Because voting rights had not yet been constitutionally granted to African Americans, thousands of people were disenfranchised.")
That vs. which	Otherwise known as the bane of every grammarian's existence, the choice to use "that" or "which" is not a matter of preference. Use "that" to introduce a clause that is essential to the meaning of the sentence (a.k.a. a restrictive clause). Use "which" with non-restrictive clauses, which add useful but not essential information. (See what I did there?)
While	"While" should be used to convey simultaneously occurring events, as in "Participants whistled while they worked." Use "whereas", "although", or "but" to convey contrast.

As an emerging researcher, you need to become comfortable using the language of your discipline. But go easy on the jargon, or loaded "code words". Like cologne, a little goes a long way and too much makes you gag. You will be taken seriously without slathering it on and, more importantly, your readers will not hyperventilate. Compare:

Jargon: Incrementally encountering to-be-remembered items increases the likelihood that contextual and semantic traces will bind in the hippocampus, entorhinal cortex, and medial temporal lobe.

English: Spacing practice improves long-term retention.

Simple. Understandable. Effective.

Rule #8 – Formatting is a Royal Pain in the Bleep, But it Matters

Bold this. Center that. Include an indent here not there. Use parenthetical expressions to cite sources.

Academics' love affair with formatting has spawned several offspring (see Table 3.2). The existence of so many formatting styles may affirm your impression that academics are intolerably anal. Let me convince you that learning a formatting style is worth your time and trouble.

Table 3.2. Common formatting styles

Discipline	Style
Communications	APA, MLA, Chicago
Criminology	APA, ASA, MLA, Chicago
Economics	Chicago, APA
Political Science	APSA, APA, MLA, Chicago
Psychological Science	APA
Sociology	ASA, APA, MLA

Note. APA = American Psychological Association; APSA = American Political Science Association; ASA = American Sociological Association; MLA = Modern Language Association

Reason #1: It makes reading scholarly work efficient and, to a certain extent, predictable. Imagine you have just eaten a great meal at your favorite restaurant. The check arrives and the first thing you see is the tax applied to the total. Next you see an entree, a drink, another entree, and a dessert in a jumble. The prices associated with these items are in a heap at the bottom of the bill. Instead of the typical format for recording prices (e.g., $10.99), you see full words (e.g., ten dollars and ninety-nine cents). Although all the information about your meal is present, you expend vast amounts of effort deciphering it because you are accustomed to the bill being arranged in a certain order (e.g., drinks, starters, entrees, desserts) and in a particular format. If the check were organized and presented in the way you expected, you would be able to read and verify the information on it very efficiently.

Reason #2: It means you are conscientious, meticulous, and professional. Schwartz, Landrum, and Garung (2012) note that mastering the format of a report can "separate the good from the great" (p. 7). Why? It demonstrates that you sweated the details. Further, you took the time – your most precious commodity – to ensure that you communicated in the format scholars use.

Reason #3: It helps you hone computer skills, especially word processing. Do you know how to make a table? Use styles? Format a hanging indent? Do you even know what one is? You will after writing your research report. To satisfactorily format your report, you must use a word processing program sophisticated enough to handle somewhat tricky formatting. Simple text editing programs such as Notepad, TextEdit, and GoogleDocs will not likely have the functionality to properly format your document.

Reason #4: It develops skills and habits needed to learn other systems of reporting (one would hope). If you are not planning to write professionally in your discipline, you may think: "I'm never going to write in this style again. Why should I sink all this time into learning it?" At some point in your career, you might have to familiarize yourself with a particular system of reporting because your employer wants things done A Certain Way. Although that Way will likely not involve a scholarly formatting style, you will still have to learn the details of that system. Thus, having mastered a formatting style may better prepare you for the challenge of learning another maybe-not-quite-so-anal one.

WRITING BUILDS CHARACTER

You may think of writing your quantitative research report as just another class assignment. But it can be a life-changing opportunity. Undertaking a project of this scope requires you to leverage and build your character.

Think of someone running a marathon. She may have been born with a naturally athletic build. She may have trained hard. But right now she's on mile 21 of 26.2. Natural, inborn athleticism or training is not going to get her across that finish line when her muscles scream and sweat pours off her body. Character will.

Paul Tough (2013) lists seven character strengths that social scientists and educators believe promote academic success.[8] They include: grit (perseverance), optimism, self-control, gratitude, curiosity, zest (passion), and social intelligence. Embracing the "truths" and following the "rules" of this chapter requires you to leverage and further develop these strengths. For example, to benefit from feedback you use social intelligence to empathize with the person delivering the feedback. You are optimistic that you can improve your work. When feedback is not as positive as you had hoped, you muster grit to press on. You use self-control to carefully evaluate and address the feedback. Finally, you express gratitude for the person taking the time and energy to deliver your feedback.

Writing a quantitative research report is an intellectual marathon. Regardless of your confidence or experience writing, you may find yourself on the verge of giving up on mile 21. Take a deep breath. Let passion and curiosity drive you. Keep sight of the goal. Stick to your plan. Dig deep and push through. Be grateful for the opportunity and to those who helped you along the way. (In case you are wondering, I tell myself these very things every time I sit down to write.)

SUMMARY AND PRACTICE

Successfully writing a quantitative research report involves putting yourself in a productive frame of mind and understanding the major tricks of the trade. It all boils down to: Write, learn, teach. Writing a quantitative report will teach you a lot about your topic… and a lot about yourself, if you let it.

For practice, examine your beliefs about intelligence and writing. Consider whether you hold more of a fixed or growth mindset. With that knowledge in mind, critically examine myths about good writing and whether you believe them. Develop your writing schedule and plan for your quantitative research report. Adapt plans and goals as necessary, but ruthlessly protect your scheduled writing time. Consider the "rules" of writing a quantitative research report. Which rule resonated with you, or inspired the most thought? Why? Which rule do you think will be the most difficult for you to follow? Why? Choose a character strength and explore how you can use it to embrace the "truths" and adhere to the "rules". Write in longhand or type your response to give shape to your musings.

NOTES

[1] Your mindset can differ across domains; you can embrace a fixed mindset in one domain (e.g., writing) and a growth mindset in another (e.g., scientific reasoning).

[2] For other myths about writing, see Boice (1990).

[3] I am indebted to Dr. Brian Osoba for this turn of phrase.

[4] For a hilarious description of this process, watch Seth Meyer interview Bill Hader: https://www.youtube.com/watch?v=kVHJc26t3Gc.

[5] For a refresher, consult Thurman (2003) for basic grammar, and Strunk and Whites's (1999) *Elements of Style* for more advanced stylistic advice.

[6] In case you are wondering, the medical terms for 4- and 6-fingeredness are "symbrachydactyly" and "polydactyly". I bet you're happy I opted for pop culture references.

[7] Your Method and Results/Analysis section also need to achieve global coherence. However, the structure of these sections is typically more prescribed than the Introduction/Literature Review and Discussion.

[8] These character strengths are derived from Peterson and Seligman's (2004) theory that posits 24 distinct, universal character strengths. Research involving the role of character strengths in higher education is in its infancy. Other character strengths such as bravery, love of learning and integrity, may predict academic success in college students (Lounsbury, Fisher, Levy, & Welsh, 2009).

WRITING A QUANTITATIVE RESEARCH REPORT

INTRODUCTION

As you learned in Chapter 3, the social and behavioral sciences have more than One Right Way of organizing a quantitative research report. Although arrangements vary, all research reports answer the following four overarching questions:

- What question did you ask (and why should anyone care)?
- What did you do?
- What did you find?
- What does it all mean (and why should anyone care)?

Chapters 4 through 7 discuss how you address these questions. Turns out you tackle big questions by answering several "smaller" ones (smaller in scope, not in importance). Your responses to these questions will appear in different sections of your research report depending on your discipline. In Section 3 you will see how some disciplines go about organizing responses to these questions.

The question-based approach I've used in this section plays to your strengths. As a student, you answer questions all the time; you know the drill. Further, it is a straightforward strategy to ensure that you include essential information in your report. But, here's the caveat (a.k.a. my recurring nightmare) – you approach your research report as you would a final exam. You carefully answer each question on a separate page. Then you mash the pages together and, *Voila*! You have your report. At this point I wake up clammy and hyperventilating. With labored breath, I croak: "Connect the dots!" These questions are not islands unto themselves; they form an integrated network of ideas. Accordingly, your responses to these questions need to form a coherent whole.

Chapter 8, cleverly titled "Odds and Ends," includes important components that supplement the major sections of your report. Many of these components are bookends, such as your title page and appendices. Other components, such as citations, are integrated throughout your report.

WHAT QUESTION DID YOU ASK?

And Why Should Anyone Care?

INTRODUCTION

Answering this overarching question "sets the scene" of your research report. You introduce your research question, provide context from existing literature, and convince your readers why your work is important. To work towards these subgoals, you need to answer the following questions:

- What is the core problem or phenomenon you have studied?
- How will you hook your reader?
- What have other researchers and scholars learned about this issue?
- What is not known about your problem or phenomenon and why is it important to fill this gap in our knowledge?
- What do you predict will happen and why?

Remember that you will learn how to organize your responses to these questions in later chapters that are dedicated to your specific discipline. So the order of these questions does not serve as an organizational blueprint, but rather as a framework to ensure that you accomplish the main goal of introducing readers to your question and convincing them to care.

WHAT IS THE CORE PROBLEM OR PHENOMENON YOU HAVE STUDIED?

Readers feel invested in your study when you identify a mutual end (Flower & Hayes, 1977). In a quantitative research report, that end is the answer to your research question. Thus, your readers need to clearly understand your research question. But before stating your question, you need to focus readers on the core problem or phenomenon that you have studied. This might be easier said than done; you may have examined several constructs, concepts, or theories. However, you need to decide upon one ring to rule them all – one core concept to anchor your report.

For example, let's say your research question was: Does using Facebook affect feelings of social anxiety (i.e., how anxious one is around other people; Mazen, Fallon, & Henkel, in preparation)? Building from the definitional hierarchy described in Chapter 1, the main constructs are social media and social anxiety. Now you could travel down two paths: You could note how social anxiety can impact social functioning, and how important it is to examine behaviors that could affect levels of social anxiety (i.e., a problem). Alternatively, you could discuss the ubiquity and rapid growth of Facebook, leading to why it is important to investigate potential socio-emotional consequences of social media use (i.e., a phenomenon).

How do you decide which concept is your core? First, consider your audience. In this case, if the audience consists of individuals interested in abnormal psychology or clinical issues, lead with social anxiety. Conversely, if your readers are more interested in media, use Facebook/social media as your core. Second, judge how much is known about the concepts or constructs under study. Favor the concept, construct, or theory that we know *less* about because that makes your research more important. If you are still on the fence after considering the first two suggestions, select your outcome or dependent variable.

Once you've decided on your core, you need to introduce it so that it leads inevitably to your research question. In other words, you need to "hook your reader".

HOW WILL YOU HOOK YOUR READER?

As usual, Zinsser (2006) is spot on:

> The most important sentence in any article is the first one. If it doesn't induce the reader to proceed to the second sentence, your article is dead. And if the second sentence doesn't induce him to continue to the third sentence, it's equally dead. Of such a progression of sentences, each tugging the reader forward until he is hooked, a writer constructs that fateful unit, the "lead". (p. 54)

Think of the best novels you've read – they likely have amazing beginnings: "124 was spiteful." "A screaming comes across the sky." "In my younger and more vulnerable years my father gave me some advice I've been turning over in my mind ever since." These openers invite you – compel you – to read on largely because they tease the theme of the novel, but do not give everything away.

Writing about your quantitative research project can be every bit as engaging, but scientists take a different approach to constructing their openers. A fictional opener creates a series of questions that the reader wants answered. Who or what is "124" and why is he, she, or it spiteful? What is a screaming and why is it coming across the sky? What's the fatherly advice and why does it provoke so many thoughts? But these questions may be red herrings for the real theme of the book. In scientific writing, the opener clearly teases your core problem or phenomenon. The ideal audience reaction after reading your opener should be, "Really? Show me." Consider McClosky's (2000) punchy hook: "Every economist knows by now that monopoly does not much reduce income. Every economist appears to be mistaken" (p. 36). She's got my attention and I want to see how she's going to support that claim.

If you would like a more tempered approach to hooking your reader, Kail (2015) provides three suggestions.[1] You could open with a familiar behavior that is poorly understood. Stand-up comics who revel in observational humor (e.g., Katt Williams, Louis C. K., Paula Poundstone) use this strategy religiously. Although comics can get away with "Ever notice how…", your approach should be more like: "Go to any family-friendly restaurant and notice how many family members are holding electronic devices." Readers can likely relate to this real-world situation and will want to read on to see whether your study confirms their expectations. This approach is especially helpful if you are studying a basic research question. This clear and practical application provides a familiar idea for readers to hold on to as they work their way through abstract theory and constructs. It also reminds you of the potential applications of your research, which will be important when you discuss what your findings mean.

A second strategy is to begin with a hypothetical situation followed by a rhetorical question, as in: "Imagine a stranger approaches you and asks you to buy her a cup of coffee. What would you do?" Readers' answers will depend on how they envision the stranger, which could launch a discussion of stereotypes or prosocial behavior. A great opener allows you to pivot to your core problem or phenomenon while teasing the other constructs you have studied.

A third approach involves opening with an interesting fact or statistic. Edwards (2012) supplies a sociological example:

Sixty-four percent of mothers of preschoolers are in the labor force (U.S Census, 2010). More than 90 percent of fathers of preschoolers are in the labor force (U.S. Census, 2000). (p. 45)

Readers see the disparity and expect the report to examine work-family related issues in mothers and fathers with young children. This approach may be particularly effective with applied research questions. Providing such context to your audience introduces the practical significance of your study and helps your audience care about your research.

Notice that none of the previous examples began: "Since the dawn of civilization/time/choose-your-historical-epoch, we have been interested in/ fascinated by/probing X". Nor did any example start, "The purpose of this paper is to examine…" Both of these opening gambits, if they can be called that, are soulless and damn your readers to purgatory. Have mercy.

WHAT HAVE OTHER RESEARCHERS AND SCHOLARS LEARNED ABOUT THIS ISSUE?

You need to situate your core problem or phenomenon in the existing, relevant scholarly literature. You use the literature to tell the story of your research question or problem. Think of it as character development – you need to describe what we know about the characters (i.e., constructs, concepts, theories) and their relationships with each other. To develop a strong literature review you need to locate relevant scholarly literature, evaluate said literature, and decide how to organize it.

Locate scholarly literature.   Scholarly literature can take multiple forms; the most common sources include books (not textbooks), book chapters from edited books, and peer-reviewed journal articles. Books and book chapters from edited books generally synthesize a wide body of literature on a topic. As such, they can provide an excellent overview of a problem, construct, or theory especially when you are first learning about it. Books and chapters also provide novel insight – they could put forth a new theory, suggest areas for future research, or identify limitations in our current knowledge.

Peer-reviewed journal articles take several forms. Some articles present a theory in great detail, possibly suggesting hypotheses that derive from said theory, and specifying contexts or situations in which the theory may explain a phenomenon. Other articles are extensive literature reviews on a topic. As with books or chapters, review articles give you a general appreciation for a phenomenon and could help you identify other relevant primary sources. Empirical articles report data collection and analysis for a specific research question (i.e., what you will do with your quantitative research project). Meta-analyses involve identifying multiple published or unpublished empirical sources on a particular topic and statistically aggregating the findings to better estimate the true effect size in a population.

How do you find literature to include in your report? Although you may be tempted to confine your search to Google Scholar, become familiar with discipline-specific search engines available in most University libraries. These databases are more likely to target credible scholarly sources. Further, the databases contain features that help you constrain your search and locate sources that are particularly relevant for your purpose. Table 4.1 lists databases within the social and behavioral sciences.

Table 4.1. Discipline-specific databases

Discipline	Database
Communications	Communication and Mass Media Complete
Criminal Justice or Criminology	Criminal Justice Abstracts
	Criminology: A SAGE Full-Text Collection
	National Criminal Justice Reference Service
Economics	Business Source Premier
	First Research
	Plunkett Research Online
	Report Linker
Political Science	CIA Factbook
	CIAO
	Country Background Notes
	CQ Press Electronic Library
	Digital National Security Archive
Psychological Science	PsycINFO
	PsycTESTS
Sociology	Social Sciences Citation Index
	SocIndex with Full Text

Note. If your project crosses disciplines (e.g., behavioral economics), you may find that the databases in other disciplines will provide helpful information

You will likely find more literature on your general topic than you could or should include in your manuscript. Locating potential sources is more art than science, and takes a fair bit of practice. Your goal is to obtain a manageable number of sources to evaluate – the sweet spot is usually between 20 and 50 "hits". If you are using a scholarly database for the first time, you would benefit from asking reference librarians for assistance. They can help you broaden or narrow your search and suggest search terms that yield more promising returns. A word to the wise: Keep a list of all the search terms you have used. If you think you have exhausted all possibilities and are still coming up short, ask your professor to suggest search terms. Showing him/

her your list will accomplish two goals. First, it can help your professor make specific suggestions for terms that you may not have considered. Second, it will attest that you made a conscientious effort to locate sources before you asked for assistance.

Of course, it's possible that very little literature directly relates to your topic. Some students come to this realization and are disappointed – how can you locate scholarly sources now? Chin up. You may be tapping into an understudied area of research, and that's extremely exciting! If you find yourself in this position, think of your search in broader terms. For example, imagine you are interested in examining stereotypes towards individuals who are internationally and/or interracially adopted (Villanti, 2016). Previous researchers investigated stereotypes towards adopted individuals in general, but no research has examined issues regarding the combination of interracial and international adoption. At this point, you would synthesize what is known about stereotypes surrounding adoption and how those stereotypes may have developed. You might also broaden your literature review to include stereotypes about race and about foreign-born individuals.

Evaluate the literature.   When you have a list of potential sources, you need to judge whether the source is relevant to your purpose. Think of the literature like a family tree. You want literature to be immediate family, not third cousins twice removed. Examine the source's title. Does it contain constructs/issues/theories that are central to what you are examining? If so, skim the abstract. Will the source provide the necessary context to understand your problem or phenomenon? If so, skim the source. For books, examine the table of contents and locate a chapter that is likely to be relevant to your purpose. Also consider examining the book's index for constructs, concepts, or theories central to your project. For book chapters and theoretical or review articles, pay particular attention to headings – they can help guide your search. For empirical articles, skim the Introduction/Literature Review and Discussion/ Conclusion. Bear in mind that you will read these sources more critically later– these suggestions are simply to help you determine whether a source is worth delving into.

Many emerging researchers want to know how much literature is enough. That depends largely on the scope of your question (i.e., the number of constructs are you studying) and how much previous research exists. You need to thoroughly substantiate your assertions without disrupting the flow of ideas. Kail (2015) suggests between one and three citations per claim; more would be overkill.

Now that you have your sources, you need to decide which information to include in your Introduction. Select information that enables your audience to develop a clear understanding of the concepts, theories, and/or issues surrounding your particular research question. For empirical articles, focus on the findings – you will soon discover whether the available research converges on a common conclusion or diverges. Sources can also provide theoretical or operational definitions for your constructs and variables. Sometimes methodological information or limitations of the study are important. All sources are not created equal and the best writers carefully consider how much and what type of information readers need to know.

To ensure that you have included relevant information in your Introduction, keep your specific research question in mind as you critically read your sources. If a source does not inform your research question or your methodology, your readers do not need to know about it. While you are reading, jot down relevant ideas, definitions, methodology, findings, and/or limitations. Write about how the source connects to your research project.

Sometimes you will find paraphrased information within a source that appears relevant to your research question. All empirical journal articles include a literature review that appears like a one-stop-shop of knowledge. You may be seduced into paraphrasing someone else's paraphrasing – it's right there, ripe for picking. However, those authors paraphrased those sources with their specific purpose in mind – a purpose that differs from yours. Remember, you are telling the story of *your* research, not someone else's. Further, those authors may not have represented others' work accurately and you may end up perpetuating an error if you "borrow" from them. Thus, you should always track down the primary source and evaluate it for yourself.

Organize the literature. Your next task is to organize your information in a coherent framework. Emerging researchers typically want to structure the literature review as a chronological laundry list, with each paragraph serving to summarize a single source. Resist this urge with every fiber of your being. Why? A laundry list places equal emphasis on each source. Some sources are more central to your purpose than others, so you should give your readers what they need – more information about the most central sources. Further, the laundry-list approach breeds redundancy. You may have identified several sources that converge on a single theme. For example, three different empirical reports might contend that women are objectified in advertisements for alcohol. Although different methods may have been used to reach that conclusion, the conclusion is the same. Synthesizing all three sources in a single paragraph is far more parsimonious than constructing three individual paragraphs that essentially say the same thing. Finally, reading summary upon summary obscures connections and critical differences between sources. Remember, your job is to make your writing accessible to the widest audience – and that involves helping your readers understand the current state of the literature.

Instead of writing a laundry list, introduce a series of characters that play a role in your research question. Start with your lead – the character that has the most connections with other characters in your story. Then introduce your supporting cast and connect them to the lead. In basic research, you might start by describing the overarching theoretical framework that underlies your study. In applied research, you might begin with the outcome variable. Let's say you are examining factors related to re-electing incumbent candidates in urban congressional districts. Your first goal would be to describe the re-election rates for incumbents in major cities across the United States. Then, you could propose factors that could predict incumbent re-election.

These characters become a network of themes and you develop these themes with your sources. It's like building a house: you build the foundation (i.e., your overarching problem that you are trying to solve), then you frame the walls that connect to each other in various ways (i.e., your themes), and finally you lay the floors, ceilings, and walls (i.e., details from your sources). To be clear, supporting your themes with evidence does not mean that you selectively include sources that support a single way of thinking. Describe competing theories or conflicting findings surrounding a phenomenon. Such conflict or ambiguity further justifies why you are conducting your research.

Move from general to specific themes. For example, imagine you are examining whether learning information about something you plan to drink affects your perception of how it tastes (see Lee, Frederick, & Ariely, 2006). In your literature review, you would start with the general theoretical concepts underlying that question (e.g., top-down processing, a theory in cognitive psychology). Next, you could describe how having prior knowledge affects one's perceptions about a wide variety of things (e.g., knowing a brand of T-shirts). You could then note how prior knowledge affects taste perception specifically for food (e.g., knowing a brand of deli meat). Finally, you could review the literature involving effects of prior knowledge on taste perception for beverages (e.g., knowing a brand of soda). To summarize: Top-down processing (i.e., having knowledge about something) affects perceptions about a lot of things, including food, and particularly drinks. General to specific.

Some writers use subheadings to provide structure and coherence to their literature review. Subheadings can substantially benefit readers when reviews are long (over 5 pages) and multiple paragraphs are integrated under each subheading. However, subheadings can serve as an organizational crutch when you cannot figure out how to transition between concepts or themes (McClosky, 2000). Subheadings may also tempt you to include tangential information that leads readers astray from your primary focus. Use subheadings with caution and incorporate them *after* you have achieved coherence through honing your topic sentences (see Chapter 3).

WHAT IS NOT KNOWN ABOUT YOUR PROBLEM OR PHENOMENON AND WHY IS IT IMPORTANT TO FILL THIS GAP IN OUR KNOWLEDGE?

Answering this question is perhaps the most potent means to convince your audience that your report is worth reading. Clearly articulate how your study will move your science forward. Specify the hole(s) or gap(s) in our current knowledge that your research project will address. In other words, scientifically justify your research.

In my experience as an instructor, emerging researchers find it challenging to articulate how their project adds to a discipline. Here are some possibilities:

- Directly replicate a published study;
- Investigate an entirely "new" or unstudied phenomenon;
- Use different measures, stimuli, or manipulations to examine a known phenomenon or test a theory (i.e., conceptual replication);
- Examine known phenomena in a different population or different time period (i.e., generation/era);
- Test hypotheses for competing theories using a single method;
- Examine relationships between variables that previously have not been linked;
- Provide additional evidence surrounding a controversy or ambiguous phenomenon; or
- Validate a new instrument (i.e., questionnaire).

Explicitly specify the new information readers will learn from your research. Then go a step further and convey why gaining this knowledge is important. For basic research, your findings would produce greater understanding of a phenomenon and support or refute a particular theory. You might also have made a creative methodological contribution. Like basic research, findings from applied research have implications for theory and general knowledge. In addition, you should clearly articulate how your findings would have real-world, practical application.

Now that you have specified the holes or gaps in readers' knowledge, describe how your study will fill them. For example, if you are testing hypotheses for competing theories, describe your method and explain why it is a good test of the theories. To examine relationships between variables that previously have not been linked, note how you obtained data for these variables through self-report questionnaires, observation, or archival sources. If you are using different measures to examine a known phenomenon, mention your specific measures and describe how they differ from previous research. In short, provide enough detail about your study for readers to understand how your research project addresses your justification for conducting it.

A final cautionary note: Your justification cannot be personal or anecdotal. You may have a deep, personal connection with your research topic. Perhaps you are examining outcomes in juvenile offenders because of direct experience or experiences of a close family member or friend. Having this connection fuels your passion and gives meaning to your work. Being deeply invested in your project is something every educator hopes for her student. But your personal experience or connection with your topic does not constitute scientific justification and does not belong in a research report.

WHAT DO YOU PREDICT WILL HAPPEN AND WHY?

Predictions are succinct, declarative expectations deriving from theory. Tell your audience what you hypothesize regarding your main variables of interest. Avoid getting bogged down in too much detail; formulate predictions using constructs or variables rather than operational definitions. Further, describe the expected nature of the effect or relationship whenever possible. For example:

> *Ideal prediction*: In married couples, a more egalitarian division of household chores should be associated with higher relationship satisfaction.

> *Not-so-ideal prediction*: In married couples, partners who split household chores (e.g., vacuuming, laundry, cooking, landscaping, etc.) 50-50 should report greater satisfaction with their relationship on the Relationship Satisfaction Questionnaire (Hendrick, 1995) than partners with a less egalitarian division of labor.

Although both predictions are declarative expectations regarding the main variables of interest, the first prediction is easier to process.

Further, ensure the language you use within a prediction is consistent with the conclusion you can draw from your research design. For example, if your project involves establishing relationships between measured variables, you should avoid using language that conveys causal connections between those variables.

Language that does not imply a causal connection: Undergraduates who qualify for Pell Grants should be less likely to graduate college in 4 years than those who do not qualify for Pell Grants.

Language implying a causal connection: Qualifying for a Pell Grant decreases undergraduates' chances of graduating college in 4 years.

In the latter case, the language implies that qualifying for a Pell Grant causes a decline in 4-year graduation rate. Perhaps another variable related to socio-economic status such as the quality of the high school students attended accounts for the entire relationship between Pell Grant status and college success. In this case, implying a causal connection would be scientifically irresponsible.

Making a prediction indicates a commitment to statistically evaluate and ultimately discuss that prediction. Do not make predictions that you have no intention of statistically analyzing. You may have noticed that predictions are worded as "alternative hypotheses" (i.e., your predictor variables should be related to your outcome variables). However, in your analysis, you will evaluate whether the null hypothesis is probably true.

Although you will statistically evaluate whether your variables are related, you should rationalize the expected relationship by explicitly connecting your predictions to theory and extant literature. As with scientific justification, predictions should *not* be made on the basis of personal experience, anecdotes, or "gut instinct". For example, you would not predict that "fiscal conservatism" is a myth in the Republican Party because your best friend, a staunch Republican, favors increasing government spending for "entitlements". Exceptional cases will always exist. Your focus should be on normative trends informed by theory and empirical findings, rather than idiosyncratic examples.

Given that predictions need to be grounded in theory and empirical findings, do not make predictions for variables or constructs that you did not introduce in your literature review. Let's say that you are interested in examining perceptions of cross-racial humor in White and Black Americans. Your literature review is chock full of scholarly sources about racial stereotype theory and perceptions of disparaging humor. On the basis of your literature review, you predict that White and Black young adults would find cross-racial humor (e.g., a Black comedian making fun of White people) funnier than same-race humor (e.g., a Black comedian making fun of Black people). Then you predict that men would find cross-racial humor funnier than women. Hold up. Where did that come from? Making that prediction would require reviewing the literature on sex differences in perceptions of humor, tolerance, agreeableness, etc.

Sometimes researchers' findings run completely contrary to their initial predictions. As an emerging researcher, resist the urge to retrofit your predictions to match your findings. If you have conducted a thorough literature review and your predictions are informed by said literature, you have done your job.

In lieu of predictions, researchers in some disciplines occasionally pose specific questions. That said, these questions perform the same general function of a prediction – they guide analysis.

A NOTE ABOUT VERB TENSE

As you were learning how to address the previous questions, you may have wondered about the nitty gritty details of verb tense. If verb tense never crossed your mind, humor me.

Use *present* tense to:

- theoretically define your core problem or constructs of interest.
- report statistics about the *current* incidence or prevalence of a phenomenon (e.g., "According to the Center for Disease Control, approximately 29 million Americans have diabetes.").
- describe a theory.

Use *past* tense to:

- convey the methodology, findings, or limitations of previous empirical research.
- describe aspects of your study (e.g., "In the current study, I examined whether stereotype threat theory explained athletes' 'choking under pressure' during sports events").

- make a prediction[2] (e.g., "I expected that playing a violent video game would increase hostility more than playing a cooperative video game"). Note that the conditional mood (i.e., "would") is used as well.

QUESTIONS ACROSS SECTIONS

You've diligently worked to answer the questions in the previous sections. Where do they belong in your research report? That depends on which overarching structure you are using – think back to the hands from Chapter 3. Table 4.2 illustrates where the responses to each question will likely live in your research report. That said, discipline-specific practices may overrule the following suggestions.

Table 4.2. Typical residences of answers pertaining to the question you asked in your research report

Question	(one hand)	(two hands)
What is the core problem or question you studied?	Introduction	Introduction
How will you hook your reader?	Introduction	Introduction
What have other researchers and scholars learned about this issue?	Introduction	Literature Review
What is not known about your problem or question and why is it important to fill this gap in our knowledge?	Introduction	Introduction or Literature Review
What do you predict will happen and why?	Introduction	Literature Review or Method subsection

SUMMARY

The beginning of your research report is an "origin story" of sorts; you describe how your research project came into being. You identify a problem or question, describe what you already know and what you don't, convince your readers that your problem was worth investigating, and predict the outcome or pose questions that you will answer later in your report. What's on the horizon? You tell your readers how you went about answering your questions.

NOTES

[1]   See Dunn (2004) and Kendell, Slik, and Chu (2000) for additional suggestions.
[2]   Note that ASA style (American Sociological Association) requests predictions in *present* tense.

CHAPTER 5

WHAT DID YOU DO?

INTRODUCTION

Time to answer questions about the nuts and bolts of your research. The goal is to provide enough information about how you conducted your study so that anyone could replicate it. In particular, you should answer the following questions:

- Who or what did you sample?
- How did you operationally define your variables?
- How did you collect your data?

Although answering these questions may feel like grunt-work documentation, the information you provide helps your reader evaluate the validity of your study. For example, describing your sample speaks to whether your sample adequately represents the population from which it is drawn (i.e., external validity). Your operational definitions detail how you measured or manipulated the variables you theoretically defined (i.e., construct validity). The manner in which you collected your data helps readers evaluate how well you minimized the impact of extraneous variables (i.e., internal validity).

Social and behavioral scientists use three major methodological approaches to obtain data. You can analyze the content of mediated messages, examine secondary data using archival datasets, or collect data from human participants. We'll discuss content analysis, archival datasets, and primary data collection with human participants[1] in turn.

CONTENT ANALYSIS

What Did You Sample?

Describe what qualifies as an element of analysis – a magazine ad, a television show, a song, a violent event in a movie, etc. Note how many elements you included in your sample.

Next, explain how you obtained and selected – sampled – these elements. If you can access all possible elements within a population, you can randomly draw from these elements. More commonly, researchers use purposive, or relevant sampling (Krippendorff, 2004). From the entire population of elements, you limit your sample to elements that possess criteria relevant to your research question. Imagine that you are examining case law for infractions of Title IX (i.e., the law prohibiting discrimination on the basis of biological sex in federally funded education programs or activities). Within a comprehensive case law database, you could search for cases involving Title IX. Then you could limit cases to those involving universities, athletic programs, and so on until you arrive at a manageable number of relevant cases to analyze. If that number is still too large, you can randomly select cases from your purposive sample.

Sometimes researchers compare elements across an important variable. Going back to Title IX case law, perhaps you want to compare the decisions of such cases within primary and secondary school settings. To ensure that the conclusions you draw are based on the school setting, you would identify other extraneous variables that might differ across the groups (e.g., the range of years the lawsuits were filed, the States in which the complaints were lodged, etc.). The more comparable your groups on these extraneous variables, the more likely your variable of interest accounts for differences between the groups.

How Did You Operationalize Your Variables?

In content analysis, operational definitions emerge within your coding scheme. Your first task is to define your basic unit of analysis (Weber, 1990). In textual elements, the unit could be words, word sense (i.e., words in context), sentences, themes, paragraphs, or whole texts. Other media, such as film, might incorporate different units. For example, Heggen (2014) examined the social construction of disability in *Buffy the Vampire Slayer*. Her unit of analysis was the episode and she coded the entire series (144 episodes) for disability-themed words (with some appreciation for word sense) and the appearance of characters with physical or mental disability.

After specifying the basic unit of analysis, define mutually exclusive categories and determine their scope. Returning to *Buffy*, Heggen (2014) defined disability language (e.g., lame, cripple, retarded, insane, etc.) and recorded the number of times such language appeared throughout the series. She noted all instances of such language; thus, the context was quite broad (e.g., "Now I have to blow my entire allowance to get this *stupid* tattoo removed."). Reference any previous literature that influenced your operational definitions. Provide enough detail so that anyone replicating your study could follow your scheme and obtain comparable results.

Although the content is important, the form a message takes can be especially revealing (Neuendorf, 2002). For example, the music video industry of the late 1980s received a fair amount of criticism regarding its portrayal of women, particularly as victims of aggression (Vincent, Davis, & Boruszowski, 1987). Yet, Kalis, and Neuendorf (1989) found that women in music videos were more likely than men to be *initiators* of aggression. But film involves more than content – camera angles and duration of images or scenes shape viewers' impressions. Female victims of aggression were on screen significantly longer than male victims. Further, female victims were more likely to be depicted in extreme close-ups than male victims. Thus, the form of the message rather than the content increased the salience of women being perceived as victims of aggression.

How Did You Collect Data?

Researchers collect data by personally coding content, using technological aids to code content, or combining the two. If you personally coded content, describe a typical coding session. How long were the sessions? How many elements on average did you code in a session? How much time, overall, did the coding take? Your audience should appreciate the care you took to produce reliable and valid data.

Technological aids are often used to help researchers code many elements efficiently. Carefully describe the program and the specific procedure you used to obtain your data. Imagine you examined how introductory sociology students incorporate functionalist theory into their term papers. Perhaps you used QDA Miner Lite to identify variations of the word "functionalist" and appearances of "Durkheim" (who is largely credited for originating this theory) in 500 elements. Notice that technological aids on their own provide a relatively crude picture of the phenomenon of interest – you might count instances of "functionalist" and "Durkheim" quickly, but important contextual elements (e.g., Did students use those terms correctly or insightfully?) would be lost. For this reason, researchers often combine personal and technological approaches to collecting data.

The major challenge in collecting data for your content analysis involves the ambiguities inherent in the messages themselves (Weber, 1990). Consequently, you should attend especially to two types of reliability: stability and reproducibility (Krippendorff, 2004). Stability refers to

77

consistency in the same coder's analysis of the same data at two or more time periods (like test-retest reliability). Reproducibility is akin to inter-rater reliability in observational studies. Here, more than one rater codes the same content. Whereas stability involves the coder's unique perspective, reproducibility assesses shared understanding between coders (Weber, 1990). Even if you are using a computer program to analyze content, you can still assess stability – you may have erred when you recorded the data from the computer output or did not set the proper parameters for analysis. So, you would reanalyze a subset of data to confirm reliability in your measurements.

SECONDARY OR ARCHIVAL DATASETS

Who (or What) Did You Sample?

Your first task is to describe the database you used to answer your research question. State the name of the database and describe who (or what) comprised the sample. Do the data represent individuals, larger groups of people (e.g., neighborhoods, cities, districts, states, regions), organizations, or products or services? How many total cases are in the database? When were the data collected?

Note the number of cases you analyzed (e.g., 5,967 registered voters, 12,563 online titles). Researchers often do not use all cases in a database; they select cases based on criteria relevant to their research question. For example, Ifcher and Zarghamee (2015) used data from the General Social Survey (GSS) to examine variation in the happiness of single mothers. They restricted their analysis to respondents 45 years of age or younger because older individuals are less likely to have children under the age of 17 living at home.

If you are comparing different groups, specify how you defined each group. Imagine you wanted to compare voter turnout across congressional districts differing in per capita wealth. You would describe how you used median household income to define three groups (low, medium, and high wealth). Although you are interested in wealth status, other extraneous variables (e.g., biological sex, race/ethnicity, registered political affiliation) might be related to wealth and consequently obscure the relationship between wealth and voter turnout. You should examine and report such differences across groups. You might statistically control for these differences or acknowledge them when you discuss your findings.

How Did You Operationalize Your Variables?

Operational definitions should be consistent with those reported by the researchers who developed the database you are using within your study. For example, the website for the General Social Survey (GSS) contains the actual questions and measures used to collect survey data (http://www3. norc.org/GSS+Website). You will not use all of the data within the database (there are 5600 variables in the GSS!) – specify variables that are relevant to answering your research question.

You may find that you want to make continuous variables in the dataset categorical. Imagine you are using the GSS to examine whether age is related to who people voted for in the 2012 presidential election. You may not be interested in slight variations between 31- and 32-year-olds. Rather, you could focus on trends across broader age-based categories corresponding to generational labels such as "Baby Boomers", "Gen X-ers", and "Millennials". Your reasons for creating categorical variable may also be statistical. If a variable of interest is bimodal (or multimodal), creating mutually exclusive categories would be a wise statistical decision. Whatever your reason, specifying categories from continuous variables is part of operationalizing your definitions.

How Did You Collect Data?

With archival data sets, you have not collected the data yourself. Your description of your dataset should incorporate information about how the data were collected. Most archival databases maintain a codebook or other such guide describing their sampling procedures and other details regarding data collection.

PRIMARY DATA COLLECTION WITH HUMAN PARTICIPANTS

Who Did You Sample?

Begin with the total number of participants in your sample. Describe how you recruited and compensated your sample. Supply descriptive statistics for important demographic characteristics (e.g., age, biological sex, and race/ethnicity).

Describe any restrictions to your sample. You may have limited your sample because of your particular research question. Let's say you are interested in students' transition to university; consequently, you restrict your sample to first-year undergraduates. You should note how many participants you excluded because they did *not* meet the criteria required for inclusion in your study.

If you have compared groups of people along an important characteristic (e.g., White and People of Color) or randomly assigned them to different experimental conditions (e.g., watching contemporary dance or Latin dance), you should report demographic characteristics across different groups or conditions. To draw valid conclusions from your study, you want to minimize the likelihood that extraneous variables (e.g., demographic variables you are not interested in) could explain the relationships or effects you found. For example, if you were comparing undergraduate men and women's performance on a difficult math task, you would want to ensure that the men and women in your sample had comparable experience with math (e.g., taken roughly the same number of math courses). You can efficiently summarize these demographic characteristics in a table. You could take your reporting a step further and conduct inferential statistical analyses to examine whether your groups are comparable.

How Did You Operationalize Your Variables?

Researchers measure variables in several ways, including questionnaires, direct behavioral observations, and physiological recordings. Researchers may also manipulate variables using stimuli. Bear in mind that your study could employ multiple techniques for manipulating or measuring variables.

Published questionnaires that measure a single construct. Describe each questionnaire in a separate paragraph and cite its source. Include the number of items and the response scale (e.g., 5-point Likert). If a questionnaire has subscales (i.e., particular items that measure more specific components of the overall construct), describe them and note how many items correspond to each subscale. For example, a 22-item questionnaire measuring sources of test anxiety could consist of three subscales: perceptions of the test, perceptions of the self, and perceptions of the testing situation (Bonnacio & Reeve, 2010). Include a sample item for each questionnaire or subscale as needed.

Report psychometric properties (i.e., validity and reliability) for each questionnaire. Seek out statistics assessing convergent validity, divergent validity, criterion validity, internal consistency, and test-retest reliability (see Chapter 1). Often, this information appears in a publication devoted specifically to the instrument's development or assessment.

Pro tip: Even if a scale has been shown to demonstrate acceptable internal consistency, you should examine that issue empirically in your own sample. Imagine you are doing a study about procrastination and you are using Lay's Procrastination Scale (Lay, 1986). The reported inter-item consistency is .82 (well above the acceptable level of .70) and the test-retest reliability is .80. Looks great, doesn't it? One of the items reads: "A letter may sit for days after I write it before mailing it." In the 21st century, I'm afraid that letter writing has become a lost art. If you used this scale with a sample of contemporary undergraduates, that item is no longer valid and would likely reduce the measure's inter-item reliability. Thus, you should always conduct your own internal consistency analysis.

Describe how you reduced scores across multiple items into a single summary statistic, or composite score.[2] For example, the Narcissistic Personality Inventory-16 (Ames, Rose, & Anderson, 2006) involves responding to one of two choices that best captures your personality (e.g., "I like to be the center of attention" or "I prefer to blend in with the crowd"). To obtain a score, researchers sum the number of "narcissistic responses". This approach works well until a participant does not respond to one or more of the items. If this occurs, you have two options: Exclude participants who do not respond to all items, or calculate an average (assuming that you have enough responses on the measure to do so).

Unlike a sum, median or mean scores fall within the range of possible points on the scale itself. So, if you calculate an average for measure with a 7-point Likert-type response scale from 0 to 6, you know the mean or median must fall between 0 and 6 no matter how many items are on the scale. Imagine there are 13 items on that instrument. If you calculated the sum, scores would range from 0 to 78, which is harder for readers to conceptualize.

Original or substantially revised questionnaires that measure a single construct. Sometimes you cannot locate a published questionnaire that adequately measures your construct of interest, so you create your own. Alternatively, you may revise a questionnaire that measures a construct in a context other than the one you are studying. Imagine you were interested in romantic jealousy deriving specifically from social media use. You find a great questionnaire assessing romantic jealousy, but it does not contain items that tap jealous feelings due to social media use or jealous behaviors enacted on social media. You may choose to alter existing items on the scale or add items to suit your purpose.

Probe your new or revised scale's construct validity. At the very least, examine internal consistency. You might pursue more advanced statistical techniques such as factor analysis. As with all questionnaires, describe how you reduced responses into composite scores.

Direct behavioral observations.   Clearly and thoroughly define physical actions or responses constituting behaviors of interest. Observations could involve recording behaviors that happen in real time or through a "physical trace" – something left behind by participants. For example, you could measure prosocial behavior by recording whether someone picked up pens that were "accidentally" dropped, or by how much money someone left in a donation box (van Baaren, Holland, Kawakami, & van Knippenberg, 2003).

Indirect behavioral measures.   Researchers can indirectly examine mental processes by asking participants to perform tasks thought to manifest that process. Measurements could include accuracy (e.g., how many words participants recall), judgment (e.g., whether faces express pride or shame), or reaction time (i.e., how quickly people respond). State the number of trials participants experienced (i.e., how many times participants could respond) and describe the nature of the response (e.g., multiple-choice test, how quickly people determined that a word conveyed something pleasant, how much money participants were willing to bet).

Physiological measures.   Social and behavioral scientists also measure physiological reactions to the environment. For example, viewing violent or suspenseful films could induce arousal, thereby increasing heart rate or body temperature. Other physiological measures, such as respiratory flow, blood pressure, or blood flow within the brain require more complex equipment to measure. Describe the apparatus used to collect these measurements.

Manipulated variables.   Thus far, all the talk about operationalizing variables has centered around measured variables. Manipulated variables also require operational definitions. Manipulations often involve altering stimuli – things that people can sense and consequently respond to. Stimuli can be just about anything – written or spoken words, stories, pictures, videos, numbers, math problems, etc.

Report the number of stimuli that participants experienced and how you obtained or selected the stimuli. If your stimuli are inspired by or obtained directly from published works or the internet, cite the author/source. You also need to describe precisely how the stimuli systematically differed (i.e., your manipulation) and how you held certain characteristics of the stimuli constant (i.e., control variables). Further, note any special apparatus you used to present your stimuli (e.g., PowerPoint projector).

How Did You Collect Data?

Report how you tested participants in a step-by-step, chronological fashion so readers can envision themselves participating in your study. If you were required to obtain ethical approval from an institutional review board to conduct your study, state that up front. Describe the setting of data collection (i.e., where the study took place) and how many participants were tested at a time. If you tested multiple participants per session, consider describing the seating arrangements/room layout. Explain how you introduced your study to participants and note how each participant read and signed an informed consent, if applicable.

Next, describe how participants experienced your materials. If participants completed a series of questionnaires, note how you ordered materials (e.g., Latin Square). If applicable, describe how you assigned participants to conditions of a manipulated variable, noting any special counterbalancing that occurred for within-participant variables.

Finally, describe how you debriefed your participants. If your procedure included deception or involved asking particularly sensitive questions (e.g., sexual behavior, drug use), explain the special actions you took to remove or alleviate potential negative aftereffects. Report how long, on average, participants needed to complete the procedure.

Studies involving naturalistic observation in public spaces do not require participants to provide informed consent or necessitate subsequent debriefing. In such cases, describe the setting(s) in which you observed participants. Note the time of day your observations took place and how many observational sessions you conducted. Carefully describe the technique you used to sample behavior (e.g., time sampling, event sampling).

A NOTE ABOUT VERB TENSE

Most of these questions will be answered using past tense. However, use present tense to describe what a published questionnaire measures (e.g.,

"The Mini-IPIP measures the Big 5 personality traits"). You might also use present tense to describe an archival database (e.g., "The General Social Survey includes over 5600 variables.").

QUESTIONS ACROSS SECTIONS

In a rare moment of cross-disciplinary harmony, all questions pertaining to "what you did" reside in the Method (or Research Design) section of a research report. However, organization within this section varies substantially across disciplines and research designs (you knew the harmony was too good to last!). Researchers typically organize information into three subsections: Participants (or Sample), Operational Definitions (Materials or Measures), and Procedure. Subsection order differs across and even within disciplines. For example, in Psychological Science, you typically see Participants, Materials, and Procedure. But it is not uncommon to encounter Participants, Procedure, and Measures in questionnaire studies. Studies involving archival data may only include two subsections detailing the sample and operational definitions. And, some disciplines do not include subsections at all, opting for a more integrated description of methodology.

Despite organizational variation, operationalize your variables in the order in which you will describe them within the Procedure or Results/Analysis. Such consistency will enhance your report's clarity and coherence. Following this suggestion can help your Method/Research Design section feel less like a runaway train and more like a high-performance sportscar.

SUMMARY

In this chapter, you worked construction. You gave readers a blueprint detailing how you selected your sample (and important characteristics of said sample), how you operationalized your variables, and how you collected your data. Now to deliver the goods: you describe what you have found after statistically analyzing your data.

NOTES

[1] Some behavioral scientists conduct research with non-human animals. But that is beyond the scope of this book.
[2] If your measure has subscales, you could calculate a composite score for each subscale.

CHAPTER 6

WHAT DID YOU FIND?

INTRODUCTION

This question is the beating heart of quantitative research – you finally answer your research question. To do so, you need to consider the following component questions:

- What was your study design and/or plan for analysis?
- How should you write about your findings?
- How should you visually represent your findings?

WHAT WAS YOUR STUDY DESIGN AND/OR PLAN FOR ANALYSIS?

Not all research reports explicitly address this question. Nevertheless, this approach is especially helpful when studies involve complex experimental designs incorporating multiple independent variables or sophisticated regression or structural equation models. For example, economists often specify stochastic equations corresponding to the "steps" in logistic multiple regression or time-series analyses used in economic forecasting. Describing your study's design and plan for analysis helps your audience bridge the gap between your data collection and your analysis.

HOW SHOULD YOU WRITE ABOUT YOUR FINDINGS?

The moment everyone has been waiting for – your findings! And yet you may feel as if you are writing in a foreign language. You're using statistical terminology and talking about data in ways that are new to you. Still, your job is to continue telling your story in a way that keeps everyone on board and engaged.

Your analysis should read like good textbook posing clear questions and subsequently answering them. Think about a textbook that you enjoyed reading (take as much time as you need). I'd wager that the textbook had a clear and intuitive overarching organization with topics flowing in a logical manner. Within the chapters and major sections, the authors of this fabulous text asked questions within a well-defined scope and subsequently answered them with sound evidence.

In short, good textbooks (and Results/Analysis sections) have strong macro- and microstructures. The macrostructure involves the overarching organization: Which question should you answer first, second, etc.? The microstructure involves constructing answers to those questions.

Macrostructure

Exploratory analyses. The purpose of exploring your data is to probe for problems that compromise subsequent analyses. The four most concerning problems for emerging researchers are: invalid data points, non-linearity of relationships, non-normal distributions of continuous variables, and outliers (i.e., data points that are not statistically consistent with the majority of the data) or points of influence.

Humans can produce invalid data. Data points have questionable validity due to: suspected response bias (e.g., participants answer "3" for all items on a questionnaire); response omissions (e.g., participants do not provide responses for a certain percentage of items or trials); participant disinterest, fatigue, or other incapacitation (e.g., being "under the influence"); or technological/experimenter error (nobody's perfect!). In such cases, you may decide to discard those data points. Note how many participants or observations you discarded and reasons underlying your decision. Clearly report how many participants or observations remained in your sample.

If you use inferential tests to determine whether your predictions convincingly reflect what occurs in the population, you need to examine whether your data meet the assumptions of these tests. Many tests are based on a linear model, so your data need to be linearly related to use such tests. Creating a scatterplot is the easiest way to determine whether the relationship between variables is linear. Some statistical tests such as regressions and MANOVAs require that variables are not too strongly related, or multicollinear. If you are using such tests, you would report correlation coefficients to quantify the strength of the relationship between predictor or dependent variables.

Many inferential tests also require your data to be normally distributed. Report statistics quantifying skewness and kurtosis and plot your data using histograms. If you are comparing groups of people and/or between-participant conditions in your study, examine normality separately in each group or condition. Imagine you are testing whether the jokes in *Big Bang*

Theory have increased in their geekiness over time. (Let's not worry about operationalizing "geekiness" for the moment!) You compare geekiness ratings for seasons 1 and 2, 3 and 4, and 5 and 6. You should ensure that the data in each of those epochs were normally distributed. If your data are not, entertain transforming your data. Report the transformation you used and the effect on the distribution. Alternatively, you can use advanced statistical techniques that produce accurate statistics despite skewed or kurtotic distributions (e.g., bootstrapping; see Field, 2013).

Be on the alert for individual data points that do not behave like the majority of the data (i.e., outliers) or unduly influence the strength of a relationship between continuous variables (i.e., points of influence or leverage). Your statistical program will likely offer multiple ways – both visual and statistical – to identify outliers and points of influence. Statisticians debate the best ways to handle outliers (e.g., Osborne & Overbay, 2004). You could report analyses with and without the discarded data, allowing readers to evaluate the discarded values' influence. Alternatively, you could conduct "robust" statistical analyses reduce the influential effects of outliers (Field, 2013).

Primary analyses. Your primary analyses address the specific hypotheses you stated earlier in your report. Ideally, you would have planned these analyses upon making your predictions and deciding upon your methodology. Before launching into your primary analyses, you may need to explain how you quantified certain variables.

Imagine you investigated the relationship between hostility in tweets and specific topics (politics, religion, movies, etc.). To quantify hostility, you assigned each tweet a rating of 0 (no hostility) to 9 (extremely hostile). After you scored the tweets, you realized that there was little "middle ground" in hostility. Tweets were either blatantly hostile or benign, resulting in a bimodal distribution. Thus, you decide to group tweets as hostile or non-hostile. If you create categorical variables from continuous measures, report the means and standard deviations for each group. For example, I would note that the benign tweet group had a mean hostility score of 2.14 with a standard deviation of 0.62.

Describing how you quantify variables is particularly important in experiments. Describe the criteria used to determine whether responses were included in analysis. For example, if you measured reaction time (i.e., how long it took participants to respond to a stimulus), you might find that participants spent a disproportionately long time responding on a few trials. People occasionally sneeze, zone out, or check out. Consequently, you may choose to discard data from such trials. For variables measuring accuracy, you should describe what constitutes an accurate response – sometimes it's not obvious. Imagine that participants freely recalled words from a list. You would describe the criteria you used to determine whether the response was accurate. Were minor spelling errors OK (e.g., "bananna" for "banana")? Would you accept plural forms of singular nouns (e.g., "cats" for "cat")? Once you've clearly described inclusion criteria, report how you reduced responses into a single score (e.g., sum, mean).

Secondary analyses.   Secondary analyses elaborate or contextualize your primary analyses. Unlike primary analyses, you do not make specific predictions regarding these analyses earlier in your report. Rather, these analyses address potential alternative explanations for the relationships or effects you observed in your primary analyses. As such, secondary analyses often occur in experimental designs.

Imagine you examined whether listening to particular types of music affected how efficiently young adults multitask (i.e., switch from one task to another). Music affects mood and arousal, so you might examine whether mood and arousal changed comparably across different music conditions or whether mood and arousal levels were correlated with multitasking efficiency. You also might assess participants' familiarity with the music they heard. If participants were more familiar with a certain type of music, you have identified a confound in your experiment.

Secondary analyses may involve manipulation checks to ensure that your manipulation operated as intended. Let's say you examined how sadness affects perceptions of helping behavior. You induced sadness by asking participants to write, in detail, about the saddest event of their life. To ensure that participants actually felt sad, you would assess their emotional state before and after the induction. Further, you would evaluate whether degree of sadness correlated with perceptions of helping behavior.

Microstructure

Now that you have a sense of the broad elements of analysis, we should address the minor detail of writing about specific analyses. Your description of any analysis should include four major components: (1) the hypothesis (or research question); (2) the analysis you used; (3) which variables were incorporated in the analysis and the role each played (e.g., independent, dependent variable); and (4) the finding(s).

Predictions/Research questions. The cardinal rule of writing a strong analysis section is to let your predictions (or research questions) drive your organization both globally and locally. After all, you are conducting analyses to test predictions. As such, reiterating the purpose of the analysis seems a logical starting point for a paragraph. Let's say you examined factors that predicted female undergraduates' decision to major in a STEM discipline. You might begin, "To examine factors that predicted female undergraduates' probability of majoring in a STEM discipline…"

Analysis. Once you have reminded your readers of the purpose of the analysis, identify which analysis you conducted to test the prediction or research question. Continuing on from the example above: "…I conducted a probit regression…"

Variables. Now you're cooking. After stating the statistical analysis you have used, clearly state the variables in question and their roles. Following the example above, "…using mother's college major, Math SAT, and high school science GPA as predictor variables." Of course, the way you describe and label your variables depends entirely on your specific analysis. Imagine you investigated whether online blogging reinforced content and improved students' performance on a subsequent midterm (Lindberg, 2015). You might write:[1]

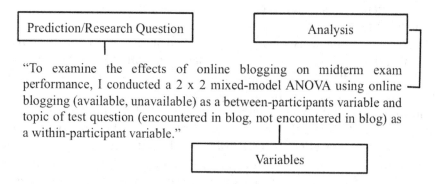

Findings. To effectively describe your findings, you need to: (1) communicate the direction and magnitude of the relationships or effects; (2) telegraph whether the relationships or effects were statistically significant (i.e., your model provided a good fit to the data); (3) support your interpretation with descriptive and inferential statistics, and refer readers to a table or figure if applicable; (4) note the importance of the model using effect size statistics; and (5) convey whether your findings support your predictions.

That's a lot of information and a straightforward example is in order. Let's return to the question of predicting young women's participation in STEM majors in college. We'll simplify the question to whether having a mother who majored in a STEM discipline is associated with participation in STEM. I would write:

> To examine whether having a mother who majored in a STEM discipline is associated with a women's participation in STEM programs, I conducted a 2 × 2 chi-square test of independence. As expected, students whose mothers majored in STEM were more than twice as likely to participate in STEM programs (75%) than students whose mothers did not (35%), χ^2 (1, $N = 134$) = 8.25, $p < .001$, $\phi = 0.25$.

Note how I accomplished all five goals within the second sentence. Go ahead and marvel in wonder and admiration – I don't mind. Realize that more complex analyses would require additional deconstruction (i.e., more sentences).

Two additional questions emerge when you are reporting findings: First, how should you report analyses with transformed data? You conducted the analyses with transformed data, so report the inferential statistics from these analyses. Note that transforming data alters the original units of your measurement. Thus, researchers often report descriptive statistics both in text and in tables and figures using original, non-transformed data.

Second, what happens when you conclude that there is no relationship or effect, or that your model poorly fits the data (i.e., null effects)? Historically, statistics for null effects have not often appeared in the scholarly literature. However, discipline-specific style guides have begun calling for these statistics. This shift belies a deeper appreciation of the limitations of null hypothesis testing and the importance of effect size. If you have a large enough sample, any effect or relationship will be statistically significant. But your effect size may be paltry, or quite unimportant in the grand scheme of things. Conversely, your test statistic may have almost been large enough for you to reject the null hypothesis, but your study did not have enough statistical power. Nevertheless, your effect size is reasonably healthy. If your sample is representative, then that effect should hold with more observations (Cummings, 2013). Thus, omitting null results may artificially downplay important effects or relationships. I advocate reporting null results – it is good practice.

HOW SHOULD YOU VISUALLY REPRESENT YOUR FINDINGS?

You've heard that "a picture is worth a thousand words". That adage literally proves true in your research report. (OK, maybe not 1000 words worth, but you get the idea.) Providing visual representations of your findings in tables or figures is helpful for at least two reasons. First, you summarize a lot of information efficiently, reducing your audience's fatigue and confusion. Second, you highlight what you consider to be key findings in tables and figures. If all of your findings are embedded within your prose, your readers may not appreciate the importance of particular findings over others. In short, tables and figures harness attention.

Tables

Tables summarize scads of statistics. You can report descriptive statistics for several groups or conditions in a glance. In addition, tables can organize findings for complex statistical analyses, such as ANOVAs or regressions. Imagine if you had to incorporate all that information in written prose! That would be cumbersome for you as well as your reader. Tables free you to highlight main points in your prose and help readers more easily digest your analyses and findings.

Histograms

Histograms visually depict the frequency distribution of values along a single variable (see Figure 6.1). Rather than represent the frequency of each potential value, histograms "bin" values, condensing several values into a range of scores. Histograms clearly capture skew, kurtosis, or multimodality in a distribution. Further, histograms depict outlying data points. Thus, you can use histograms to support many analytic decisions, such as transforming the data to achieve a normal distribution, creating categorical variables out of continuous variables, and identifying and potentially discarding outliers.

Scatterplots

Scatterplots illustrate the relationship between two continuous or discrete variables (see Figure 6.2). You can discern many important things from scatterplots including linearity, direction, strength, outliers or points of influence, and the impact of third or moderating variables.

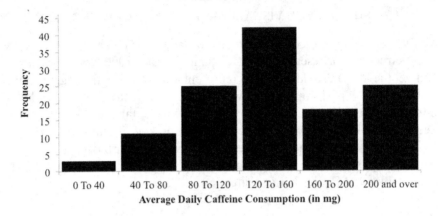

Figure 6.1. Histogram illustrating average daily caffeine consumption

If the points in your scatterplot appear to travel upward from left to right, you have a positive linear relationship (as values of one variable increase, so does the other). Points giving the impression of moving downward from left to right represent a negative linear relationship (as values of one variable increases, values of the other decrease). The direction of the relationship is particularly clear if the scatterplot includes the least squares regression line (or "line of best fit"), which minimizes the distance between it and all other points in the distribution.

Scatterplots also give readers information about the strength of the relationship. The steepness of the slope of the least-squares regression line does not exclusively determine the strength of the relationship. You need a non-zero slope for a relationship to exist, but the distance between observed points and the predicted values specified on the least-squares regression line determines the strength of a relationship. The closer points in the distribution are to the line of least squares, the better fit (stronger relationship).

Outliers or points of influence stick out like a sore thumb on scatterplots. In Figure 6.2, one point does not look like the others: Someone drinks about 450 mg of caffeine on average and is not very anxious, which bucks the positive trend between caffeine intake and anxiety.

Scatterplots can also help you discern whether you have a third-variable problem or a moderating variable. Third-variable problems arise when it looks like you have a relationship between two variables, but the association is completely explained by another variable. In Figure 6.3, the overall

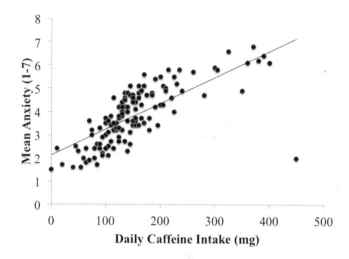

Figure 6.2. Scatterplot illustrating the association between daily caffeine consumption and anxiety

correlation between anxiety and caffeine intake is strong ($r = .68$). However, this relationship can be explained almost entirely by biological sex. Women (in this fabricated sample) are generally more anxious and caffeine-loving than men. Examining the least squares regression lines within men and women reveal that the positive association between anxiety and caffeine intake is not as strong as it is for the entire sample. Thus, the strong relationship between caffeine intake and anxiety would be considered spurious, or illusory.

Additional variables are not always this problematic. Sometimes variables exert a moderating effect on the relationship of interest; the overall trend is still present, but the strength of the relationship differs across levels of the additional variable. In Figure 6.4, that association between caffeine intake and anxiety is stronger for men than for women, despite the fact that men seem to have lower caffeine intake and anxiety than women on average. In this case, we would say that biological sex moderates the relationship between caffeine intake and anxiety.

Bar and Line Graphs

Bar and line graphs typically illustrate one or more categorical variables functioning as independent or predictor variables and one continuous variable representing a dependent or outcome variable.[2] The dependent

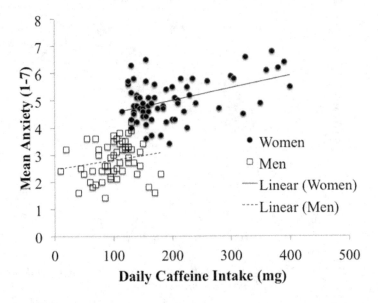

Figure 6.3. Scatterplot illustrating the association between daily caffeine consumption and anxiety with biological sex as a third-variable problem

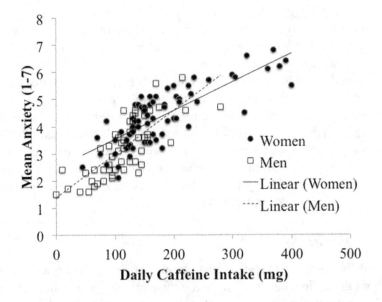

Figure 6.4. Scatterplot illustrating the association between daily caffeine consumption and anxiety with biological sex as a moderating variable

variable commonly appears on the Y axis, whereas independent variables are represented on the X axis and within the legend. The height of the bar or the position of the marker in a line graph corresponds to the mean (usually) of that condition or group.

So if we return to our caffeine and anxiety example, suppose you divided participants into three groups according to their caffeine intake (low, moderate, and high). Now caffeine would be a categorical variable and can appear along the x axis (see Figure 6.5). You would consider caffeine intake an independent variable. Anxiety, as a continuous variable, is represented on the y axis; it is your dependent variable. Biological sex is represented within the legend and is a second independent variable. Thus, the height of the bars represents the mean anxiety levels for men and women across the different levels of caffeine intake.

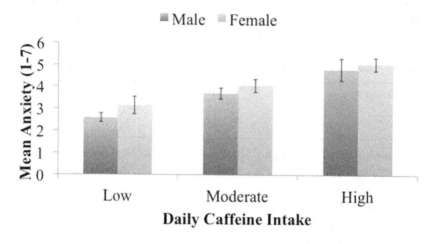

Figure 6.5. Bar graph illustrating an interaction between daily caffeine consumption and biological sex. Error bars represent 95% confidence intervals

Remember that mean differences alone do not help you determine whether a difference in your sample accurately reflects a difference in the population. So that readers can make this determination in a glance, include error bars around the means. These error bars look like whiskers that extend above and below each mean. They can represent standard error of the mean or 95% confidence intervals; report this in your figure's caption.

In Figure 6.5, the nonoverlapping 95% confidence intervals show us that mean anxiety significantly increases across levels of caffeine intake. But this pattern is slightly different for men and women. At moderate and high levels of caffeine intake, men and women report comparable levels of anxiety (the 95% confidence intervals overlap considerably). However, at low levels of caffeine intake, women appear to report higher levels of anxiety than men (the 95% confidence intervals overlap very little).

Table and Figure Placement Within Your Research Report

In all major formatting styles used in the behavioral and social sciences (APA, APSA, ASA), tables and figures appear after the references or bibliography. See Chapter 8 for more details.

QUESTIONS ACROSS SECTIONS

Answers to the previous questions can appear in up to three different sections of the research report, depending on your discipline. Table 6.1 illustrates where your responses might live.

Table 6.1. Typical residences of answers for what you found

Question		
What was your study design and/or plan for analysis?	Method or Results/ Analysis	Method or Results/ Analysis
How should you write about your findings?	Results/Analysis	Results/Analysis
How should you visually represent your findings?	Results/Analysis	Results/Analysis

THOUGHTS ABOUT WRITING

If you are reporting many analyses, use subheadings to help your readers remain focused. Subheadings could include headings used in this chapter (i.e., Exploratory analyses, Primary analyses, Secondary analyses). Alternatively, you could use elements of your hypotheses as subheadings (e.g., Biological sex as a moderator of anxiety and caffeine intake). Regardless of your approach, remember your goal: your audience needs to understand the answer(s) to your research question(s).

Reporting analyses can sound formulaic (ironic, I know). As you move from analysis to analysis, you may begin to use the same sentence structure, emphasizing clarity over style. Once you've clearly stated the findings work to reduce boilerplate. Why not be clear *and* engaging while reporting numbers?

SUMMARY

You started with questions and now you have answers. You helped your readers navigate a sea of statistical analyses using an effective macrostructure, clear microstructure, and illustrative tables and figures. You stated whether your data support your predictions, but that's just a tease. Now you explain what it all means.

NOTES

[1] If you included a detailed design/proposed analysis section in your report, you may not need to provide such detailed information about your analysis here.

[2] Bar graphs aren't limited to continuous data; they can also represent frequencies for categorical data.

97

WHAT DOES IT ALL MEAN?

And Why Should Anyone Care?

INTRODUCTION

No, you haven't materialized an existential philosophy course. In this chapter, we move beyond reporting findings and wrestle with what your findings mean for society and for science. To this end, you need to answer the following questions:

- How do you explain your findings?
- What are the limitations of your study?
- Where do you go from here?
- What are the broader applications of your research?
- What is your take-home message?

Notice how the now familiar subtitle "And Why Should Anyone Care?" graces this chapter. Here is another opportunity to convince your audience that your study is worth reading.

HOW DO YOU EXPLAIN YOUR FINDINGS?

Explanations begin with your main findings. Then, connect your findings to existing literature and theory and examine your findings from multiple angles. Sounds straightforward until you realize that studies have three possible outcomes. Your findings support your predictions, do not support your predictions, or partially support your predictions. Let's tackle strategies for explaining each outcome.

Your Data Fully Support Your Predictions

First, take a moment to bow your head and thank the universe – you have won the quantitative research lottery. Next, remind readers of the theoretical and empirical groundwork underlying your predictions. Tell your audience how your findings "fit" within this broader context.

Even though your findings support your predictions, entertain alternative explanations. If your study involves measured variables, consider third variables that could explain relationships. In experiments, question whether confounding variables account for effects.

Why should you explore alternative interpretations? Wouldn't exposing alternatives detract from your findings? Nope! Exploring potential explanations demonstrates that you have thought deeply about your data and are not blindly committed to a single explanation. Interpretational monogamy does not move science forward. Try out several partners and cozy up to the explanation with the best fit… and dreamiest eyes.

Your Data Do Not Support Your Predictions

If your data do not support your predictions, you either found null results or statistically significant findings that ran counter to what you expected. Let's tackle null results first. Although your findings did not align with the existing literature, remind your readers of this literature. Focus specifically on the literature that justified your predictions, including the theory from which you derived predictions. Next, interrogate your null effects. Statistically speaking, null results can occur because: (1) there really is no relationship between those variables in the population; (2) you have too little between-group variance (i.e., your signal is too small); or (3) you have too much within-group variance (i.e., your noise is too large).

There really is no relationship between the variables of interest. Making this argument is a gutsy move, especially if the existing literature and theory led you to confidently expect a statistically significant relationship between your constructs. Stating that the relationship really does not exist flies in the face of that rationale and suggests that the theory requires substantial revision.

It is entirely possible that extant literature contains spurious relationships or has overestimated the strength or statistical significance of relationships. After conducting a large-scale replication of 100 studies published in top-tier psychological science journals, Brian Nosek and his colleagues (2015) reported that only a third of the replicated effects were statistically significant and the effect sizes were roughly half as strong. Although this study examined research in psychological science, the lesson likely holds true for all social and behavioral sciences. Thus, the existing literature may present a biased view of the strength and fidelity of a given relationship.

If your study adds to a growing literature of inconsistent findings, the theory may indeed require an overhaul. Nevertheless, you should dig deeper into your own methodology and consider other reasons why you did not detect the predicted relationships.

You have too little between-group variance. Between-group variance reflects systematic variation within your measurement (a.k.a. the signal). Null effects can emerge because differences between the groups or conditions you compare are too subtle. Imagine you examined whether you could instill false memories in eyewitness accounts of a crime by providing confirmatory reinforcement. When eyewitnesses described the crime, you replied to half of them with "I see" (control) and the other half with "Yes, tell me more" (confirmatory). Although some eyewitnesses may have thought that the confirmatory response validated their recollection, it may not contrast enough with the control response ("I see") to elicit a significant difference in false memory. Responding with "Another eyewitness made the same observation" is a much stronger operational definition of confirmatory reinforcement and would be more likely to produce variation in responses.

The sensitivity of your measures could also account for weak between-group variation. For example, asking whether someone would or would not cheat on an exam is a rather broad distinction. Providing only two options for responding precludes distinctions such as definitely would cheat compared to probably would cheat. Put another way, the measure may be accurate, but it is imprecise. You are more likely to find variation between groups using more precise, or sensitive measurements.

You have too much within-participant variance. Within-participant variance is also known as unsystematic variance, or noise. The most likely culprit is uncontrolled extraneous variables (i.e., variables that are not central to your purpose). Such variables can take several forms: participant, researcher, environmental (or situational), or measurement.

Behavioral and social scientists hope that participants' responses accurately reflect their thoughts, emotions, or behaviors. But you may not catch participants in optimal states. They can be distracted, sick, hungry, tired, sad, mad, etc. Pre-existing conditions or characteristics may also affect participants' responses. For example, participants who forgot their reading glasses may become especially fatigued when filling out a series of questionnaires. Further, participants' unique experiences or knowledge may increase within-participant variance. Imagine you are examining reading comprehension and you use widely available practice passages from the SAT (Scholastic Aptitude Test). Some participants may have had direct experience with those passages or already know something about the content within those passages.

In the case of primary data collection, researchers can unwittingly increase within-participant variance through their behavior and characteristics. Dressing unprofessionally or acting disinterested or aloof may signal that you do not care about your study. If you don't care, why should participants? Encouraging some, but not other participants to do their best or pay attention will also inflate within-participant variability.

Environmental or situational variables can also affect participants' responses. In many cases of primary data collection, the testing environment can be reasonably controlled or at least monitored. The temperature and lighting of a testing room can be held constant. Noise and distractions can be minimized (hopefully!). However, collecting data online relinquishes a fair amount of control over the testing environment.

Sometimes the manner in which stimuli or questionnaires are presented increases within-group variation. Ideally, you want all participants to experience stimuli or questionnaire items in the same manner. Imagine you presented a series of images designed to elicit happiness. You would ensure that all images are equally sized, are presented using the same photographic filter (sorry, Instagram), and appear within the same medium (on paper or presented through a projector). With questionnaires, you would make sure that the typeface is clear and large enough to read easily.

You can never completely eradicate within-participant variance when humans supply data. Even in content analyses, within-participant variance can creep into measurements when humans make subjective judgments about content. Science involving humans does not happen in a sterile environment or in a vacuum. As such, you need to stomach some mess.

Your Data Partially Support Your Predictions

Like a teen breaking curfew, you have a lot of explaining to do. Partially supported predictions are murky and often require you and your audience to tolerate ambiguity. The strategies listed in the previous sections can help you navigate these seas of possibility. Remember to connect your findings to existing literature and explore alternative explanations. On the upside, partially supported predictions provide fertile ground for future research!

Your Findings Run Counter to What You Expected

Explaining your findings just got even more interesting. Counterintuitive results can turn current thinking on its head. But before you start expecting a call from Nobel, you want to – say it with me – explore alternative explanations. Assuming that your counterintuitive findings are accurate, you need to develop informed explanations. Some reasons might be methodological (e.g., you sampled from a different population, you used different stimuli or measurements). Also consider theoretical possibilities: Do known phenomena or theory explain your unexpected results?

WHAT ARE THE LIMITATIONS OF YOUR STUDY?

All quantitative research is limited in some way; yours is no exception. Explaining your findings may involve addressing some of your study's methodological limitations. In addition to exploring your study's internal validity, consider whether your measures are reliable and valid (construct validity), your sample is representative (external validity), and your conclusions have strong statistical support (statistical validity).

Are your Measures Reliable and Valid?

Reliable and valid measures speak to the construct validity of your study. If you conducted a content analysis, examine inter-rater reliability and turn a critical eye to the coding scheme or method you used to quantify your variables. Were your operational definitions too broad or too narrow?

If you used published questionnaires, you likely examined their psychometric properties before conducting your study. Nevertheless, you should examine these properties, particularly inter-item reliability, within your own sample.

With archival data sets, you have no control over selecting the measures. Still, you can comment on their validity and reliability. Perhaps you discovered a more recently published instrument that would better measure a construct.

Is Your Sample Representative?

Even when your data fully support your predictions, your findings may not necessarily generalize to the population of interest (i.e., have external validity). Researchers ensure representativeness through their sampling techniques. If everyone within a population has an equal opportunity to participate in your study (i.e., random sampling), your sample will be representative of population. However, social and behavioral scientists often recruit participants who are readily available (i.e., convenience samples or purposive samples), which could result in a biased sample.

You may assume that the larger your sample size, the more likely your sample will accurately reflect the population. But large samples can be biased – it depends upon the sampling technique. Small samples could accurately represent the population if participants are randomly sampled.

To address concerns about your sample's representativeness, compare relevant demographic characteristics from your sample to the population. If your sample is comparable to the population, you can argue that your sample is representative. (It's still possible that you did not account for an important demographic variable that differs across your sample and your population.) Further, keep in mind that representativeness of the sample is more concerning for applied or translational research than for basic research (Morling, 2015).

Do Your Findings Have Strong Statistical Support?

Sometimes we get hung up on p value; we blindly chase that coveted p of .05 or less. An overemphasis on p values leads emerging – and some seasoned – researchers to think, "If only I had a larger sample! I would have had enough statistical power to detect the expected relationship." This is absolutely true. If you sampled 10,000 people, you would likely obtain a significant p value. But the relationship may not be terribly meaningful.

As you have learned, effect sizes provide an important index of the strength, or meaningfulness of a relationship. Many effect size statistics are independent of sample size. So, even if you obtained "null results" based on p values, examine your effect size. Medium or even strong effects may emerge despite lackluster p values. Conversely, relationships with "significant" p values may have small effect sizes.

Further, data in social and behavioral science research are often messy. Humans are complex beings; consequently, they produce data far from ideal. Acknowledge when your data violate assumptions underlying statistical tests and describe how you sanitized your data by removing outliers or influential data points.

A Word of Caution about Limitations

Emerging researchers can easily get wrapped up in documenting limitation upon limitation. But don't let that undermine the value of your research.

Your research, flawed though it is, still shapes our current understanding of a topic. Avoid giving voice to every little thing that is wrong with your study. Select the most important points that readers would find insightful and have the most promise of moving science forward.

WHERE DO YOU GO FROM HERE?

One of the amazing things about being human is our ability to project ourselves into the future and be hopeful (Lopez, 2013). Your research study is one piece in a vast puzzle; you can shape what the puzzle looks like now and in the future. What's next?

Future directions emerge organically from limitations. Should someone attempt to extend your findings in another context or to a different population? Should someone address the methodological issues that arose as you were conducting your study? The more insightful the limitation, the more exciting the potential for future study.

Surprising or counterintuitive findings beg for future study. Obtaining data from an open source website, a team of researchers examined 3200 selfies from people living in five major world cities (http://selfiecity.net/). They found head tilt is quite common in selfies, but is surprisingly more pronounced in women to the tune of 50%. Although these data have not been published in a scholarly peer-reviewed source, they are an excellent example of how surprising findings can inspire future research, even across disciplinary boundaries.

Your findings might naturally point to the next logical step needed to solve a problem or understand a phenomenon. Your study has gotten us one link farther in a long chain of research. What's the next link? Take the plunge – shape future science.

WHAT ARE THE BROADER APPLICATIONS OF
YOUR RESEARCH?

Science contributes to the public good. Explore how your findings might apply outside of your specific context. Who might use your findings and how might they apply them in the real world? Municipal school board members or state legislators might your use research on the economics of local public schools to inform funding decisions. Educators might use your research on adaptive strategy use to enhance their students' learning. Non-profit organizations might use your research on sociological factors underlying teen pregnancy to steer outreach programs.

Although your findings can have meaningful impact, avoid overreaching in your study's applications. Remember that your study exists within the context of other literature. Important policy decisions should not be made on the basis of a single study, but on a growing body of information. Explain how your study, within a body of literature, can be applied to solve real-word problems.

WHAT IS YOUR TAKE-HOME MESSAGE?

This is it – your entire research report culminating in a single paragraph. Your take-home message is your study "in a nutshell" (Flower & Hayes, 1977). It's the sound byte you want lingering in your readers' ears after they've read your report. And it is the reciprocal of your hook from the beginning of your report.

Although it's tempting to stalwartly focus on restating the findings, be sure to convey the *point* of those findings. Readers should appreciate how your findings inform current literature/theory, how they inspire further inquiry, and how they can be applied or extend beyond the context of your study.

Zinsser (2006) noted that "the most important sentence in any article is the first one" (p. 54). Probably the second most important sentence is the final one. Consider:

"So we beat on, boats against the current, borne back ceaselessly into the past."

"Yes, she thought, laying down her brush in extreme fatigue, I have had my vision."

"Who knows but that, on the lower frequencies, I speak for you?"

When deciding whether to give your report a thoughtful read or cursory glance, your audience will scan the first and final paragraphs of your report. Give your readers every reason to explore all that lay between.

A NOTE ABOUT VERB TENSE

As in Chapter 4, answering these questions requires a mix of present and past tense.

Use *present* tense to:

• entertain alternative explanations for your findings.

- suggest directions for future research (e.g., "Future research should replicate these preliminary findings."). Note that the condition mood (i.e., "should") can be used.
- examine how your findings relate to theory (e.g., "These findings support social strain typology.")
- describe the implications of your research.

Use *past* tense to:

- reiterate your findings.
- describe previous empirical findings.

QUESTIONS ACROSS SECTIONS

By and large, the answers to the previous questions appear in the Discussion section of a research report. However, a conclusion section (i.e., the six-fingered approach) adds spice. Table 7.1 illustrates where the responses to each question might live in your research report.

Table 7.1. Typical residences of answers for what your findings mean

Question		
How do you explain your findings?	Results/Analysis or Discussion	Results/Analysis or Discussion
What are the limitations of your study?	Discussion	Discussion
Where do you go from here?	Discussion	Discussion or Conclusion
What are the broader applications of your research?	Discussion	Discussion or Conclusion
What is your take-home message?	Discussion	Conclusion

SUMMARY

You have explored how your findings add to our existing knowledge, inform theory, are limited, shape future lines of exploration, and can be applied to real-world contexts. You answered questions and opened the door for more. Your audience leaves your report satisfied, yet hungry. Before the sun sets on your research story, you must attend to some odds and ends.

ODDS AND ENDS

INTRODUCTION

We have detailed the major players in a quantitative research report. Now we attend to the supporting roles, most of which bookend the major sections of your report. The Title Page and Abstract appear before your Introduction. In-text citations appear within the body of your research report. References (also called Works Cited or Bibliography), Tables and Figures, and Appendices follow the final section of your report (i.e., the Discussion or Conclusion).

TITLE PAGE

Like a birth announcement, the title page announces your study. The title is your audience's first encounter with your project, so carefully consider names for your baby. Titles should be short and informative. In 15 words or fewer, readers should understand the major constructs you've investigated.

Avoid traditional title traps, including the "The Effect of X on Y" and "The Relationships Between X, Y, and Z in Q". Kail (2015) also recommends shunning clever-but-too-cute titles that rely on readers' knowledge of pop culture. Consider a recent criminology article: "Smells Like Teen Spirit: Evaluating a Midwestern Teen Court" (Norris, Twill, & Kim, 2011). The song *Smells Like Teen Spirit* is timeless, but it came out 20 years before this article. Construct a title that teases your take-home message: "Increasing Sanctions in Teen Court May Lead to Greater Recidivism and Drop-Out Rate". (This was actually Norris and colleagues' conclusion – you'd never know it from their title.)

As proud parent of your project, your name and institutional affiliation follows the title. Depending on your formatting style, you might also include: word count; contact information for the corresponding author (that's you); acknowledgments, or who you would like to credit or thank (that's me – just kidding); and potential conflicts of interest (e.g., your funding source, if applicable). Title pages generally have specific formatting requirements, so carefully review your discipline's preferred style guide.

ABSTRACT

The abstract briefly summarizes important elements of your project in one paragraph ranging from 150 to 250 words, depending on your styling format. Think of all the abstracts you skimmed while attempting to locate literature for your project. The most effective abstracts focused you on critical features of the study, contained tight and crystal clear prose, and enticed you to read on.

Write the Abstract after you've drafted the bulk of your report – you can't summarize your study without knowing what you've said. Lead with the purpose of your study and why your topic was important to investigate. Briefly describe how you studied your research question. List your major findings and convey the broader implications of those findings. How did your findings move your science forward or apply to people outside of your study's sample? Avoid the lazy final sentence: "These findings are discussed in light of the …".

Resist the urge to "dump" your knowledge and sound smart in the abstract. Make it as easy as possible for readers to figure out whether your work is relevant to their purpose or interesting enough to peruse. Aside from the title, the abstract is your reader's initial contact with your project – and your first opportunity to hook your audience.

IN-TEXT CITATIONS

Quantitative research – or any research for that matter – emerges from previous discoveries and musings. Consequently, you need to carefully document your sources. To get a sense of how seriously academics take referencing, note the number of pages devoted to proper citation format in any of the disciplinary style guides (APA, ASA, APSA, MLA). It's stunning. Hence, we turn our attention to in-text citations and references.

In-Text Citations

In-text citations occur within the body of your research report. The majority of formatting styles used in the social and behavioral sciences employ parenthetical citations[1] using an author-date citation system. Authors' names and date of publication (usually the year) appear within the citation. This form of citation applies for journal articles, books, and articles in the popular press that have a clear author. The term "author" also applies to groups of people or organization that identify themselves under a single name (e.g., Association for Psychological Science [APS]).

MLA is an exception to the author-date rule – include authors' names and page numbers within every citation. When you cite the same author for multiple works, you include the title of the work within the citation.

In-text citations can occur as *forethoughts* or *afterthoughts*. Forethoughts use authors as nouns (often as subjects) within sentences. You cannot extract these citations from the sentence without ruining its meaning. Afterthoughts occur at the end of a phrase, clause, or sentence. Removing an afterthought citation would not compromise its meaning (but plagiarism would be a problem!). Let me illustrate using APA style:

Forethought citation: Fallon (2016) noted that students can cite published works using "forethought" and "afterthought" citations.

Afterthought citation: Students can cite published works using "forethought" or "afterthought" citation formats (Fallon, 2016).

Are there "rules" for using forethoughts and afterthoughts? Neither format is inherently better than the other. Nevertheless, certain cases seem to favor a format. Use forethoughts to draw particular attention to a source or to highlight a contrast between sources. Use afterthoughts to improve the flow or clarity of the text or to support a statement using multiple sources.

The key to properly formatting in-text citations rest upon five questions:

- How do I list authors?
- How do I separate authors from publication years?
- When do I use the word "and" or an ampersand?
- When do I use the abbreviation "et al."?
- When (and how) do I include page numbers?

We'll tackle each of these questions in turn. See Table 8.1 for forethought and afterthought citation examples across formatting styles.

How do I list authors?   Use authors' surnames. When citing a co-authored source, authors' surnames appear in the order listed on the source or within the database you used to locate the source. Do not rearrange authors' surnames in alphabetical order within a citation. For sources with three or more authors, separate author names with commas. Include initials of authors' given names only when two or more authors have the same surname and you need to distinguish them. If you are citing multiple sources within an afterthought citation, order the sources alphabetically by the primary authors' surname and separate sources with semicolons.[2]

How do I separate authors from publication years (or page numbers)? If you thought that the rules governing comma usage within prose were anal, sit back and bask in the glow of comma usage within citation formats. APA is the only citation format that requires a comma between the final author of a source and the publication year. APSA, ASA, and MLA use no punctuation to separate the final author and publication year (or page number).

When do I use the word "and" or an ampersand (&)? In co-authored sources, authors form a list. If you are using APSA, ASA, or MLA, include the word "and" before the final author. APA is a different story (again) – use the word "and" within forethought citations and an ampersand within afterthought citations. None of this matters if you are using the abbreviation "et al.", which leads us to...

When do I use the abbreviation "et al."? "Et al." is short for "et alia", or "and others" in Latin. This shortcut saves you the trouble of writing out names of multiple authors. Simply type the surname of the first author, and follow that with "et al.". Be mindful of your periods when using "et al." – placing the period after "et" or not including one at all may send your professor into equal measures of apoplectic shock and fitful rage.[3]

Things get really interesting when you have more than two authors. The rules for APSA and MLA are most straightforward: If there are four or more authors, use "et al.". ASA is more nuanced. Always use "et al." with four or more authors; start using "et al." with three authors after you've cited them the long way once. APA rules were invented to keep therapists in business. For sources written by three to five authors, use "et al." upon the second reference. Always use "et al." with six or more authors.

When (and how) do I include page numbers? With MLA, you always include page numbers within in-text citations. Other citation formats require page numbers only when directly quoting a source. The page number(s) appear(s) after the year of publication. Link page ranges with a hyphen; do not insert spaces around the hyphen. And that's where the similarities end. In APA, include an abbreviation for the page number(s) (p. or pp.). APSA requires no abbreviation or punctuation. ASA wants publication year and page number separated by a colon with no spaces.

At this point, you wouldn't be surprised to learn that there are more rules about citing particular types of sources (e.g., government documents, court

Table 8.1. Examples of forethought and afterthought in-text citations and citation rules across formatting styles

Style	One Author	Two Authors	Three Authors	When to Use "et al."	Page Numbers
APA	Fallon (2016) (Fallon, 2016)	Fallon and Smith (2016) (Fallon & Smith, 2016)	Fallon, Smith, and Jones (2016) (Fallon, Smith, & Jones, 2016)	3 to 5 authors, starting with 2nd reference; 6 or more authors, starting with 1st reference	Fallon (2016, p. 232) or Fallon (2016, pp. 232–233)
APSA	Fallon (2016) (Fallon 2016)	Fallon and Smith (2016) (Fallon and Smith 2016)	Fallon, Smith, and Jones (2016) (Fallon, Smith, and Jones 2016)	4 or more authors, starting with 1st reference	Fallon (2016, 232–233)
ASA	Fallon (2016) (Fallon 2016)	Fallon and Smith (2016) (Fallon and Smith 2016)	Fallon, Smith, and Jones (2016) (Fallon, Smith, and Jones 2016)	3 authors, starting with 2nd reference; 4 or more authors, starting with 1st reference	Fallon (2016:232–33)
MLA*	Fallon…(32) (Fallon 32)	Fallon and Smith… (32) (Fallon and Smith 32)	Fallon, Smith, and Jones… (32) (Fallon, Smith, and Jones 32)	4 or more authors, starting with 1st reference	Fallon (232–233)

Note. I have made up these references for illustrative purposes.

*If you cite the same author (or groups of authors) for multiple works, you include the title of the work within an MLA citation. A book appears as: "Fallon... (Writing Up Quantitative Research in the Social and Behavioral Sciences 232)" or "(Fallon, Writing Up Quantitative Research in the Social and Behavioral Sciences 232)". When citing articles, encapsulate the article's title within quotes and do not italicize.

cases, electronic media, etc.), secondary citing, and citing multiple works by the same author(s). This chapter is intended to help you cite the most common sources within the social and behavioral sciences (i.e., journal articles, books, and book chapters in edited books). For more specialized in-text citations, refer to a publication manual or reputable online source such as https://owl.english.purdue.edu/.

References [APA, ASA], Bibliography [APSA], or Works Cited [MLA]

After the hullabaloo over in-text citations, you may wonder why you need more references following your Discussion or Conclusion. References are detailed citations that help your audience locate sources that influenced your research. Let's first list the important elements that appear within each source type. (Note that the order of these elements will differ across formatting styles.)

- *Journal articles.* Author(s), publication date, title of article, title of journal, volume, issue (depending on formatting style), page number, digital object identifier (depending on formatting style).
- *Books.* Author(s), publication date, title of book, location and name of publishing house.
- *Book chapter.* Author(s) of the chapter, publication date, title of chapter, page numbers, title of edited work, editor(s), location and name of publishing house.

As with in-text citations, different formatting styles uniquely accomplish the goal of referencing. Again, the key to properly formatting references rests upon knowing the answers to several questions:

- How do I list authors within a single reference?
- Where do publication years occur?
- When do I use the word "and" or an ampersand?
- When do I use the abbreviation "et al."?
- What do I capitalize?
- Do I enclose titles in quotation marks?
- What information is italicized?
- What punctuation and abbreviations do I use?
- How do I specify the location of the publishing house?
- Do I include digital object identifiers (doi's)?

Table 8.2 contains examples for each source across formatting styles.

Table 8.2. *Examples of journal article, book, and book chapter citations across formatting styles*

Style	Journal Article	Book	Book Chapter
APA	Fallon, M., Smith, A. B., & Jones, C. D. (2016). The magic of confidence intervals. *Journal of Supreme Awesomeness, 2,* 125–130. doi: 123.4567.89	Fallon, M., Smith, A. B., & Jones, C. D. (2016). *The magic of confidence intervals.* New York, NY: Awesome Publishers.	Fallon, M., Smith, A. B., & Jones, C. D. (2016). The magic of confidence intervals. In M. Fallon (Ed.), *Statistics for the win* (pp. 125–130). New York, NY: Awesome Publishers.
APSA	Fallon, Marianne, Anna B. Smith, and Caliope D. Jones. 2016. "The Magic of Confidence Intervals." *Journal of Supreme Awesomeness* 2 (2): 125–30.	Fallon, Marianne, Anna B. Smith, and Caliope D. Jones. 2016. *The Magic of Confidence Intervals.* New York: Awesome Publishers.	Fallon, Marianne, Anna B. Smith, and Caliope D. Jones. 2016. "The Magic of Confidence Intervals." In *Statistics for the Win,* ed. Marianne Fallon. New York: Awesome Publishers, 125–30.
ASA	Fallon, Marianne, Anna B. Smith, and Caliope D. Jones. 2016. "The Magic of Confidence Intervals." *Journal of Supreme Awesomeness* 2(2):125–130. doi: 123.4567.89	Fallon, Marianne, Anna B. Smith, and Caliope D. Jones. 2016. *The Magic of Confidence Intervals.* New York: Awesome Publishers.	Fallon, Marianne, Anna B. Smith, and Caliope D. Jones. 2016. "The Magic of Confidence Intervals." Pp. 125–130 in *Statistics for the Win,* edited by M. Fallon. New York: Awesome Publishers.
MLA	Fallon, Marianne, Anna B. Smith, and Caliope D. Jones. "The Magic of Confidence Intervals." *Journal of Supreme Awesomeness* 2.2 (2016): 125–130. Print.*	Fallon, Marianne, Anna B. Smith, and Caliope D. Jones. *The Magic of Confidence Intervals.* New York: Awesome Publishers, 2016. Print.	Fallon, Marianne, Anna B. Smith, and Caliope D. Jones. "The Magic of Confidence Intervals." *Statistics for the Win,* Ed. Marianne Fallon. New York: Awesome Publishers, 2016. 125–130. Print.

Note. I have made up these references for illustrative purposes. But I wish the Journal of Supreme Awesomeness *actually existed.* APA, APSA, and ASA identify the medium of the source.

*MLA always specifies the medium of the source. APA, APSA, and ASA identify the medium when it is not a print source.

Once you have listed all references, organize them alphabetically using the primary author's surname.[5] Further, format them using a "hanging indent" where the first line of each reference is flush left with subsequent lines indented.

How do I list authors within a reference? As in in-text citations, you preserve the order of authorship contained in the original source. The tricky parts involve knowing when to invert surnames and given names and when to use initials for given names. APA is consistent across source types. You always put surnames before initials of given names (first or middle). For APSA, ASA, and MLA, you invert the first author's surname and given name, but not subsequent authors. Moreover, you write out the given name of all authors and include middle initials when applicable.

These rules change when you list the editor of a book. Across all formatting styles, given names appear before surnames. APA and ASA require initials for given names; APSA and MLA expand first names.

Where do publication years occur? In APA, ASA, and APSA, publication years follow the author(s). In MLA, publication year follows information about the publication outlet.

When do I use the word "and" or an ampersand? When the title of a publishing outlet contains an ampersand (e.g., *City & Community*), you keep it. But when it comes to authorship, ampersands are the whimsy of APA. They connect the final and penultimate author (or editor) in all cases except...

When do I use the abbreviation "et al."? Only MLA and APA have explicit rules about using "et al." within references. MLA gives researchers the option of using "et al." for three or more authors. APA specifies using "et al." only with eight or more authors. In such cases, you list the fist six authors, include an ellipsis (...), and list the final author.

What do I capitalize? Here, too, APA is the odd man out. Titles of articles, books, and book chapters in APA are capitalized using sentence case, where only the first word, proper nouns, and words after colons and em dashes are capitalized. However, journals are listed in Title Case, in which content, or principal words are capitalized and function words (e.g., articles, prepositions, conjunctions) are not.[4] All other formats use Title Case for all titles of articles, book chapters, books, and periodicals.

Do I enclose titles in quotation marks? In APSA, ASA, and MLA, encapsulate the titles of articles or book chapters in quotes; journal articles or book titles do not appear in quotations. APA shuns quotation marks around all titles.

What information is italicized? Book titles and journal titles are italicized across every formatting style. APA also italicizes the volume number of journals.

What punctuation and abbreviations do I use? Get ready to open Pandora's Box. The differences across formatting styles and source types are so numerous that I will highlight questions that you should ask yourself:

- Do parentheses encapsulate publication year?
- For journal articles, how are volumes, issues, and page numbers handled? Do I include spaces between these elements?
- How is the editor within an edited book specified? Do I use an abbreviation for "editor"?
- How do I handle page numbers within an edited book? Are they in parentheses? Do they include an abbreviation for page numbers (pp.)?

How do I specify the location of the publishing house? APA always specifies the state (or province/country if not the US) along with the city of the publisher. The other formatting styles require the state (or province/country) only when the city is not "well known" (by whose standards, I'm not sure...).

Do I include digital object identifiers (doi's)? APA and ASA require doi's when they are available for journal articles. These appear at the end of the reference and are preceded by "doi:". (Be wary of ever-well-intentioned software that automatically capitalizes the "d".)

TABLES AND FIGURES

Bring tables and figures to readers' attention within the text. Beginning a sentence with "As illustrated in Figure 1" immediately draws readers' attention to a powerful visual summary of the data. Despite mentioning tables and figures directly in the text, you make readers hunt for them on separate pages at the end of the report.[6]

117

Be particularly mindful of formatting guidelines for tables and figures. Should you use Title Case for axis labels? Should the figures be black-and-white? Are headings in tables set off by lines?

Each table or figure includes a title or caption that provides enough information for readers to understand your data. One approach is to briefly describe the information in the table or figure: "The association between self-esteem and the number of hours people watch *Jersey Shore*." Here, you leave the audience to form their own conclusions about the data. Alternatively, your caption could read like a headline telegraphing your interpretation: "Self-esteem is positively related to the number of hours people watch *Jersey Shore*". (The power of downward social comparison!) Select an approach consistent with your formatting guidelines. In figure captions, note what statistic error bars represent (e.g., 95% confidence intervals).

Additional information about tables can appear in notes. For example, you could designate certain symbols to reflect particular p values (e.g., $*p < .05$). Other notes might specify particular information within the table (e.g., "standard deviations appear within parentheses").

APPENDICES

Appendices typically include your materials (e.g., coding scheme, questionnaires, stimuli) and/or supplemental findings (e.g., additional figures or tables not explicitly reported within your Results/Analysis). If you collected primary data, your instructor may request your informed consent form, debriefing materials, or IRB approval documentation. Letter appendices in ascending order and, like tables and figures, refer to them explicitly within the body of your research report.

SUMMARY

Writing the major sections of your research report oriented you towards the big picture, but the devil is in the details. Preface your report with an engaging title and abstract, include immaculate in-text citations throughout, and wrap it up with carefully formatted references, tables and figures, and appendices. Congratulations, emerging researcher! Your report is complete.

NOTES

[1] Chicago style uses two citation systems: the author-date system and the "notes and bibliography" system. In this book we will focus only on the author-date system.

[2] ASA also permits chronological ordering of multiple sources as long as the author remains consistent throughout the manuscript (ASA, 2010). Some formatting styles suggest separating sources with commas in certain contexts. Here is an example from the *Style Manual for Political Science* (APSA, 2006): (Confucius, 1951; see also Gurdjieff, 1950, Wanisaburo, 1926, and Zeller, 1914).

[3] Why there is so much fuss around periods? Why abbreviate "alia"? In Latin, "alia" is a neutral gender form of "other". Technically, you could have a bunch of all-male "others" (i.e., "alii") or all-female "others" (i.e., "aliae"). So, the abbreviation "al." takes care of all permutations. You will remember this moment when you graduate from your program and you're wondering whether to call yourself an alumnus or alumna – you'll just settle on "alum".

[4] In APA, Title Case has the additional rule that any word that is four of more letters – even if it is a function word (e.g., that) – is capitalized. To my knowledge, that rule does not exist in the MLA, ASA, or APSA manuals.

[5] In MLA, if there are two works by the same author(s), don't list the author(s) on the second reference. Instead, include three dashes where the name(s) should be.

[6] One exception is in APSA style – for review purposes, APSA requests tables and figures be placed within the text. However, accepted manuscripts need to include tables and figures on separate pages at the end of the report.

EXAMPLES OF QUANTITATIVE
RESEARCH REPORTS

Do you remember my recurring nightmare? You've conscientiously answered all of the questions in Chapters 4 through 7 but the report doesn't "hang together" – you haven't connected the dots. Can I effectively describe how to create an integrated research report? Perhaps. But I would rather show you.

Undergraduate emerging researchers wrote the sample papers included in Chapters 9 through 11. They, like you, struggled within their quantitative research methods class to produce coherent, informative, and meaningful work. And they spent multiple hours in revision.

The three samples broadly illustrate how social and behavioral scientists tackle writing a quantitative research report. Consequently, the papers reflect the three major methodological approaches in social and behavioral science: content analysis, secondary data analysis, and primary data collection. Further, the papers showcase different disciplines (Political Science, Sociology, and Psychological Science) and the finger-lickin'-good organizational conventions (The Simpson, The Humanoid, and The Count Rugen).

I adapted students' papers in two important ways. I adjusted content to illustrate certain strategies I presented in earlier chapters (e.g., interrogating counterintuitive or unexpected results). Further, I reformatted the papers using three of the four major formatting styles highlighted in this book (APSA for Political Science, ASA for Sociology, and APA for Psychological Science).

To save space, I did not perfectly replicate all aspects of each formatting style. Let me highlight the major differences:

- *Title page.* I included only the title of the paper and the author. You should examine how your formatting style specifies institutional affiliation and other information, including contact information, funding, and acknowledgements.
- *Abstract.* Some style guides require word count or keywords with the abstract; I included neither. Further, some style guides require that abstracts appear on the title page.

- *Line spacing.* I used single spacing throughout the sections with additional spacing between sections and headers to help your eyes parse the major sections and subsections of the paper. All formatting styles require double-spacing and most do *not* incorporate additional spacing between sections.
- *Page numbers and running heads.* These are non-existent in the samples; look them up!
- *Figure and table placement.* To improve readability, I included figures and tables where they would most logically appear within the narrative. Depending on your formatting style, you might place them at the end of your manuscript.
- *References.* References should be the same point-size as the rest of the manuscript (typically 12-point font). The point-size included in the sample papers is considerably smaller.
- *Pagination.* Some formatting styles call for page breaks following the abstract and other sections of the research report.
- *Appendices.* No appendices are included.

Even if these sample papers do not derive from your home discipline, they illustrate how the concepts and strategies included in earlier chapters manifest across contexts. The exterior features may be different, but the heartbeat is the same. Think of songs that you can't help but move to – or at least tap a finger or foot to. Rhythmic patterns that balance complexity and predictability make people want to dance (Witek, Clarke, Wallentin, Kringelback, & Vuust, 2014). It doesn't matter if it's Ray Charles, Pharrell, Mark Ronson, or Aretha Franklin; you dance because your body wants to fill the space between the beats (Doucleff, 2014). That's what these sample papers do – in their unique way they find the optimal space between predictability and complexity so readers can get their groove on.

CHAPTER 9

CONTENT ANALYSIS

INTRODUCTION

Mr. Cory Manento conducted this content analysis within the discipline of Political Science. Political scientists study how political systems originate, develop, and operate. Analysis can extend to governments, policies (including legislation), political institutions, and political behavior. Mr. Manento used textual analysis to examine Supreme Court decisions of the "exclusionary rule", a law stating that evidence collected in violation of one's constitutional rights may be inadmissible in a court of law. The study beautifully illustrates content analysis at the word level and adds a dimension of time to capture the evolution of the Court's thinking (and politics). It is formatted using APSA and illustrates the six-digit Count Rugen organizational structure.

SAMPLE PAPER

The Ideological Shift of the Supreme Court in Fourth Amendment
Exclusionary Rule Cases
Cory Manento
Central Connecticut State University

Abstract

In 1914, the Supreme Court recognized the exclusionary rule as an essential constitutional remedy to protect citizens from illegally seized evidence in court (*Weeks* v. *United States*). Subsequently, the Court extended the exclusionary rule to the States in *Mapp* v. *Ohio* (1961). The Court appears to have shifted to the ideological right on this issue, carving out exceptions to the rule. In 1984, the Burger Court created the "good faith" exception in *United States* v. *Leon*. The even more conservative Roberts Court created the "knock-and-announce" exception in *Hudson* v. *Michigan* (2006), and made exceptions for police error in *Herring* v. *United States* (2009). To confirm the rightward trajectory of modern exclusionary rule jurisprudence, I analyzed the content in the majority and dissenting opinions in these five cases. The findings reveal a somewhat consistent shift from viewing the exclusionary rule as a constitutional right to a court-ordered remedy.

Introduction

You are a college student attending a State University and you reside in an on-campus dormitory. You have signed a contract with the University acknowledging that the University reserves the right to inspect your room at any time for contraband (e.g., candles, toaster ovens, alcohol, etc.) in plain sight. You placed a small bottle of alcohol in your bottom desk drawer, which you closed fully before you left for Winter Break. During room inspections, the inspector accidentally kicks the drawer, opening it and revealing the alcohol. The University schedules you for a disciplinary hearing and potential expulsion. Can the University legally initiate disciplinary hearings based on this search and seizure?

The Fourth Amendment to the United States Constitution protects people's right to be secure in their "persons, houses, papers, and effects against unreasonable searches and seizures," and says that "no Warrants shall issue, but upon probable cause, supported Oath or affirmation, and particularly describing the place to be searched, and the persons or things to be seized." The Supreme Court applied the exclusionary rule to Fourth Amendment cases as a legal protection for citizens that could face criminal penalties because of illegally obtained evidence. Nolo's Plain-English Law Dictionary defines the exclusionary rule as: "A rule of evidence that disallows the use of illegally obtained evidence in criminal trials." In other words, the rule prevents the government from using most evidence gathered in violation of the Constitution.

Over the past century, the applications of and exceptions to the exclusionary rule have been challenged within the Supreme Court. Further, since 1972, Supreme Court decisions have been predominantly conservative, with the most extreme conservative rulings occurring since 1991 (Martin & Quinn, 2002, 2014). Three important cases on exclusionary rule jurisprudence have come before the Court following this ideological shift to the right: *United States* v. *Leon* (1984), *Hudson* v. *Michigan* (2006), and *Herring* v. *United States* (2009). Two other landmark cases occurred before the shift: *Weeks* v. *United States* (1914), *Mapp* v. *Ohio* (1961). All five cases contain the original application of the exclusionary rule, the major expansions and exceptions made to the rule, and the rule's current state. Thus, the purpose of this paper is to analyze the content of the majority and dissenting decisions in these cases and examine whether the ideological shift of the Court is manifest in the language of these decisions.

Literature Review

Two main areas of literature are relevant to this research: the Supreme Court's interpretation of the exclusionary rule and the methodological effectiveness of word quantification and the use of words as data. Before describing legal scholars' interpretation of exclusionary rule jurisprudence, I present the facts of each case under study and the Court's rulings.

Supreme Court Rulings

In *Weeks*, police entered the home of Freemont Weeks without a search warrant and seized potentially incriminating papers. The police used these papers as evidence to convict Weeks of transporting lottery tickets through the mail. In a unanimous decision, the Supreme Court ruled that the actions of the police violated Weeks's constitutional rights. In this first application of what would come to be known as the "exclusionary rule," the Court did not allow evidence seized by police without a warrant to be used in court proceedings. In his majority opinion, Justice Day reasoned that allowing private possessions to be seized without a warrant and then used as incriminating evidence would devalue the Fourth Amendment to the point that it "might as well be stricken from the Constitution."

The Court's decision in *Mapp* was another milestone ruling supporting the exclusionary rule. Police entered Miss Dollree Mapp's home without a warrant, and when she asked them to produce one, they handed her a folded blank sheet of paper. After a struggle, the officers forcibly took Mapp to her bedroom while they searched her entire home. Inside a trunk in Mapp's basement, the officers found illegal obscene materials. Mapp was convicted of possessing obscene materials and the case eventually was appealed up to the Supreme Court. The State of Ohio argued that the seizure of evidence was not illegal, and that, even if it was, the State was not obligated to exclude the evidence from Mapp's criminal proceedings. An earlier case, *Wolf* v. *Colorado* (1949), had determined that the exclusionary rule did not apply to the States. In a 6-to-3 ruling in favor of Mapp, the Supreme Court overturned its previous decision in *Wolf* and applied the exclusionary rule to the States. The Court reasoned that the exclusionary rule was necessary to deter police misconduct. As such, this remedy must apply to state and local governments. Speaking for the majority, Justice Clark wrote that the "ignoble shortcut to conviction left open to the State tends to destroy the entire system of constitutional restraints on which the liberties of the people rest." Thus, Mapp's conviction was overturned and illegally obtained evidence is now inadmissible in State courts.

The Court created a major exception to the exclusionary rule in *Leon*. Acting on an anonymous tip, the police launched a surveillance investigation on Alberto Leon. Based upon information collected from the investigation, the police applied for a warrant and were granted one. Subsequent searches produced large quantities of drugs and other incriminating evidence. Leon was indicted for federal drug offenses. At issue was whether the affidavit for the search warrant was sufficient in establishing the probable cause necessary to obtain the warrant. The lower courts concluded that the evidence was too weak to justify a warrant in the first place. The Supreme Court agreed, but still decided that the evidence found in the subsequent search was permissible. In a 6-to-3 decision, the Supreme Court ruled that there is a "good faith" exception to the exclusionary rule. According to the majority, the societal costs of applying the exclusionary rule in this case outweighed the benefits. Justice White reasoned that the magistrate was the one at fault for issuing the warrant, so the exclusionary rule would not have a deterrent effect on the police because they would continue to defer to the magistrate's judgment. Therefore the police could act on the good faith of the warrant they were issued courtesy of the anonymous tip.

The Roberts Court created another exception to the exclusionary rule in *Hudson*. Booker T. Hudson was convicted of firearm and drug possession following a police search of his home. Although the police had a warrant, they had not followed the Fourth Amendment's "knock-and-announce" statute stating that police must wait at least 20 seconds after knocking and announcing their presence before entering a home. In a 5-to-4 decision, the Supreme Court ruled that evidence should not be excluded for "knock-and-announce" violations. Borrowing from Justice White's opinion in *Leon*, Justice Scalia's majority opinion stated that "the societal costs of applying the exclusionary rule to knock-and-announce violations are considerable." Moreover, the majority ruled that the purpose of the knock-and-announce rule was to prevent violence, damage to property, and violations of privacy, rather than to prevent police from conducting a valid and warranted search. Justice Scalia stated that adequate alternative methods existed to deter police from committing knock-and-announce violations (e.g., civil suits, internal disciplinary sanctions). Therefore, the "knock-and-announce" rule was not needed to deter police from conducting illegal searches and seizure.

The final exception to the exclusionary rule occurred in *Herring*. Police arrested Bennie Herring, subsequently searched his vehicle, and found methamphetamine and a gun. Herring argued that the evidence should be excluded because the police had arrested him on an expired arrest warrant. The expired warrant had not been removed from the police department's computer system. In another 5-to-4 decision, the Court held that the evidence was admissible. Chief Justice Roberts's opinion again stressed that "[t]he principal cost of applying the rule is, of course, letting guilty and possibly dangerous defendants go free," which outweighs the benefits of applying the exclusionary rule in these cases. Furthermore, the defendant's Fourth Amendment rights were not offended because they were the result of an isolated incident of error, rather than "systematic error or reckless regard for constitutional requirements." Thus, seizures resulting from police error that were nevertheless conducted in good faith are another exception to the exclusionary rule.

Scholarly Debate Surrounding the Exclusionary Rule

The exclusionary rule is widely regarded as an essential remedy for Fourth Amendment violations. Since the rule's application to the States in *Mapp*, it has become a topic of controversy among legal scholars and judges. Criminals can escape punishment when evidence is excluded. Thus, the rule can be unpopular with law enforcement and the general public.

Despite its unpopularity, the exclusionary rule has persisted because of its essential role in enforcing the Fourth Amendment. As Justice Clark stated in *Mapp,* without the exclusionary rule, the Fourth Amendment's guarantee against unreasonable searches and seizures is nothing more than "an empty promise." Yet after *Mapp*, exceptions to the exclusionary rule became more common as the makeup of the Court turned more conservative.

In 1979, Justice Rehnquist argued that reassessing the exclusionary rule was long overdue (*California* v. *Minjares*). Rehnquist urged his colleagues to consider to what extent, if at all, the rule should be retained. Subsequently, the conservative Burger Court created the "good-faith" exception just 5 years after Rehnquist's plea.

More recently, the more conservative Roberts Court has created additional exceptions. Maclin and Rader (2012) note that the Roberts Court has adopted the Burger Court's argument that the exclusionary rule is not an individual right anchored in the Fourth Amendment, but rather a court-created remedy that does not effectively deter police misconduct. These scholars note that Justice Kennedy, widely thought of as a moderate judge, is quite conservative on this issue. Kennedy has *never* voted to impose the exclusionary rule in a Fourth Amendment case. Even when Kennedy was a judge on the Ninth Circuit, he voted against applying the exclusionary rule in *Leon*. In his dissent in *Leon*, Kennedy lamented that "[w]hatever the merits of the exclusionary rule, its rigidities become compounded unacceptably when courts presume innocent conduct when the only common sense explanation for it is ongoing criminal activity." Justices Scalia and Thomas have been reliable conservatives on nearly every issue since they have been on the Court, including the exclusionary rule. Similarly, Justice Alito has voted conservatively regarding the exclusionary rule. Indeed, Alito and Chief Justice Roberts served in the Reagan-era Edwin Meese Justice Department, whose primary goal was to attack exclusionary rule (Bandes, 2009). During that time, Roberts found himself engaged in "a campaign to amend or abolish the exclusionary rule," when he was a young lawyer in the Reagan Administration (Liptak, 2009).

Clearly, the current Court's findings regarding the exclusionary rule have swung toward a more conservative application of the law. To better understand this ideological shift, it is important to analyze the content of the majority decisions and dissents.

Content Analysis of Court Ideology

Laver, Benoit, and Garry (2003) estimated the policy positions of political parties by quantifying words used in the political texts. Pioneering a "language-blind" word scoring technique, the group successfully replicated previous data on the parties' policy positions. The group also analyzed legislative speeches and achieved similar success. Although court decisions represent shifts in ideology, a potentially richer understanding of ideological change involves examining the rhetoric used within the majority and dissenting decisions.

Clearly, Supreme Court decisions are not the same as stump speeches or other political texts intended to persuade or instantiate a particular message. Nevertheless, Rice (2012) determined that issue codes of Supreme Court opinions were predicted through content analyses of the words used within the opinions. Further, McGuire and Vanberg (2005) argued that there is great value in estimating the Court's relative policy positions by quantifying words within opinions.

The Present Study

To date, no study has examined the Court's relative policy position on the exclusionary rule by quantifying words within the opinions. Given that more exceptions to the rule have occurred in recent years, particularly within the Roberts Court, exclusionary rule opinions offer an excellent opportunity to examine the Court's shift to the ideological right.

Research Design

The intent of this research project is to expose patterns in the rhetoric used in five Supreme Court cases regarding the exclusionary rule. The majority opinions in *Weeks* and *Mapp,* and the dissenting opinions in *Leon, Hudson,* and *Herring* were designated liberal opinions. The dissenting opinion in *Mapp* and the majority opinions in *Leon, Hudson,* and *Herring* were categorized as conservative opinions. Note that *Weeks* was a unanimous decision, and did not have a dissenting opinion.

I chose the word as my unit of analysis. Specifically, I examined content words (nouns, proper nouns, verbs, adjectives, or adverbs) rather than function words (articles, conjunctions, interjections, prepositions, etc.). Different forms of content words, such as past tense or plural, were considered one word. Words that express the same idea (i.e., synonyms) were recorded as one word (e.g., "officer" and "policeman"). However, words that are similar but express different ideas (e.g., "exclude" and "exclusionary") were counted as distinct words.

Using an online word frequency counter, I calculated the 30 most frequently used words in each opinion. Then, I selected particular words that conveyed political ideology and examined the frequency of those words across the opinions. After examining the most frequently used words in each opinion, I focused on the following words and their variants: "Constitution", "privacy", "right" (as in one's constitutional right, not ideology), "deter", and "cost".

I predicted a shift in viewing the exclusionary rule as a constitutional right and necessity to a court-created remedy. Over time, I expected words connoting civil liberties (i.e., "Constitution", "right", and "privacy") to decrease and words connoting criminal deterrence (i.e., "deter" and "cost") to increase. Further, I expected liberal opinions to address civil liberties more frequently than criminal deterrence and the opposite patter for conservative opinions.

Analysis

My hypotheses were partially supported. As illustrated in Figure 1, "constitution/al/ality" was frequently used in the *Weeks* (0.61%) and the *Mapp* liberal majorities (0.72%), and sharply declined in the conservative

Leon majority (0.04%), a trend that continued in the remaining opinions. Further, even in minority liberal dissentions, the use of the word decreased from 0.5% in *Leon* to 0.15% in *Herring*. By the final decision, mention of the Constitution was virtually indistinguishable between the majority conservative (0.09%) and minority liberal opinions (0.15%).

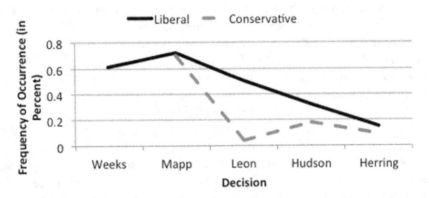

Figure 1. Variants of "constitution" across Supreme Court decisions.

This pattern was mirrored in variants of "privacy" (Figure 2). In *Mapp*, he liberal majority decision mentioned privacy much more frequently (0.41%) than the conservative majority of (0.02%). Across liberal minority dissents, mentions of privacy decreased to just 0.04% in *Herring*. Notably, the conservative majority in *Herring* did not address privacy at all.

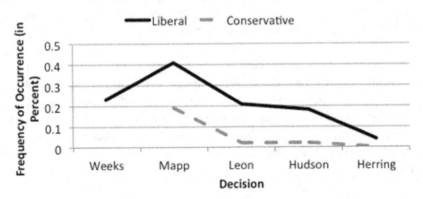

Figure 2. Variants of "privacy" across Supreme Court decisions.

Variants of "right" (Figure 3) decreased drastically from liberal majority opinions (0.58% and 0.64%) to minority opinions, especially for the case of *Hudson* (0.16%). Mention of "rights" within conservative majority or minority opinions varied relatively little (0.13% to 0.29%). Unexpectedly, the conservative majority in *Hudson* (0.29%) addressed "rights" more frequently than the liberal minority (0.16%).

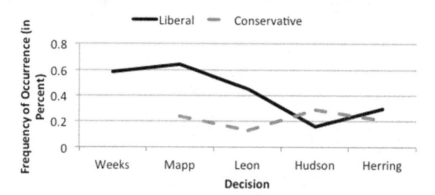

Figure 3. Variants of "right" across Supreme Court decisions.

For words conveying punishment (Figure 4), the general pattern was reversed. Variants of "deter" increased across cases, especially within conservative majority decisions. In *Mapp*, there was hardly any mention of "deter" (0.03% or 0.06%), whereas in *Herring*, the conservative majority (0.54%) and liberal minority opinions (0.38%) addressed deterrence more frequently.

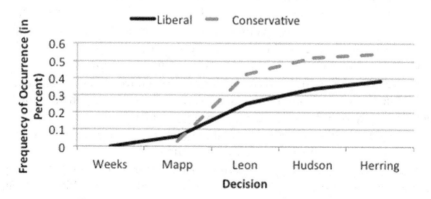

Figure 4. Variants of "deter" across Supreme Court decisions.

Variants of "cost" displayed a somewhat comparable progression with a notable exception (Figure 5). "Costs" were not mentioned at all in *Weeks* or *Mapp*. However, in Leon, the liberal minority (0.27%) addressed "cost" more often than the conservative majority (0.13%). In the final two cases, the conservative majority addressed cost progressively more frequently (0.18% and 0.25%), whereas the liberal minority remained consistent (0.09% and 0.08%).

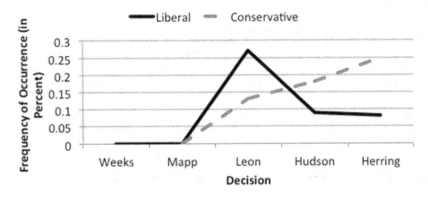

Figure 5. Variants of "cost" across Supreme Court decisions.

Discussion

My hypotheses were partially supported. Overall, the frequency of words connoting civil liberties (i.e., variants of "constitution", "privacy", and "right") decreased over time. Further, words conveying deterrence increased within the Court opinions. In most cases, changes in the frequency of occurrence were linked to the ideology underlying the opinion. Not surprisingly, conservative majority opinions containing variants of civil liberties decreased the most drastically, whereas variants connoting deterrence increased. The opposite pattern was mostly mirrored in the liberal opinions.

However, there were exceptions to these general patterns. For example, conservative opinions using variants of "right" remained relatively consistent across the five cases. Conservative opinions may have focused on the public's right to safety rather than a right to privacy. Similarly the word "cost" was very frequent in liberal's minority opinion in *Leon*. Perhaps the cost was to an individual's civil liberties rather than public safety.

Such aberrations may have arisen from dissenting opinions being written in response to majority opinions. For example, the *Mapp* dissent used "constitution/al/ality" with almost the same frequency (0.70%) as the majority (0.72%). However, this explanation does not hold within other contexts. Indeed, dissenting conservative opinions hardly mentioned variants of "privacy" (0.00%–0.02%).

Nevertheless, these opinions span nearly a century over which dramatic linguistic, technological, and legal changes that have taken place. Some observed trends may simply reflect generational changes. However, the final three cases (*Leon, Husdon,* and *Herring*) all occurred within the 21st century and increased emphasis on deterrents and decreased emphasis on civil liberties are clearly discernible.

The research design of this study is limited in three ways. First, examining frequency of word occurrence must be limited to reasonably long opinions. Justice Breyer's dissenting opinion in *Herring* is only a few hundred words long. As such, some words that may have displayed greater variation in longer opinions show relatively little variation in shorter opinions. Further, my procedure of calculating frequency does not take into account negative usages or the context in which words appear. Third, I selected the five words of interest by examining the frequencies of all of the words that appeared in the decisions. My findings may have differed had I decided *a priori* upon words to target.

Conclusion

The present study supports the contention that the ideology of the Supreme Court on the exclusionary rule has been shifting to the right, especially recently. The Court has made several exceptions to the rule, making it more difficult for defendants to be protected from unreasonable searches and seizures. Recent majority opinions argue that the societal costs of applying the exclusionary rule outweigh the benefits of deterring police from committing Fourth Amendment violations. Should this trend continue, the exclusionary rule may be swept away as a court-ordered remedy rather than upheld as a constitutional right. Lock your drawers.

References

Bandes, Susan A. 2009. "The Roberts Court and the Future of the Exclusionary Rule." Paper for the American Constitutional Society for Law and Policy.

California v. Minjares. 1979. 443 U.S. 916.

Herring v. United States. 2009. 555 U.S. 135.

Hudson v. Michigan. 2006. 547 U.S. 586.

Liptak, Adam. 2009. "Justices Step Closer to Repeal of Evidence Ruling" New York Times, January 31.

Laver, Michael, Benoit, Kenneth, and Garry, John. 2003. "Extracting Policy Positions from Political Texts Using Words as Data." *American Political Science Review* 97 (May): 311–31.

Maclin, Tracey and Rader, Jennifer. 2012. "No More Chipping Away: The Roberts Court Uses an Axe to Take Out the Fourth Amendment Exclusionary Rule." *Mississippi Law Journal* 81 (May): 1184–227.

Mapp v. Ohio. 1961. 367 U.S. 643.

Martin, Andrew D. and Quinn, Kevin M. 2002. "Dynamic Ideal Point Estimation via Markov Chain Monte Carlo for the U.S. Supreme Court 1953–1999." *Political Analysis* 10: 134–153.

Martin, Andrew D., and Quinn, Kevin, M. 2014. "Martin-Quinn Scores." http://mqscores.berkeley.edu/measures.php

McGuire, Kevin T. and Vanberg, Georg. 2005. "Mapping the Policies of the U.S. Supreme Court: Data, Opinions, and Constitutional Law." Presented at the Annual Meeting of the American Political Science Association, Washington DC.

Nolo's Plain-English Law Dictionary. "Exclusionary Rule." http://www.nolo.com/dictionary/exclusionary-rule-term.html

Rice, Douglas. 2012. "Measuring the Issue Content of Supreme Court Opinions through Probabilistic Topic Models." Presented at the 2012 Midwest Political Science Association Conference, Chicago.

United States v. Leon. 1984. 468 U.S. 897.

Weeks v. United States. 1914. 232 U.S. 383.

CHAPTER 10

SECONDARY ANALYSIS OF ARCHIVAL DATA

INTRODUCTION

Mr. Anthony Huaqui conducted a secondary analysis of archival data in Sociology. Sociologists attempt to understand human social behaviors through the lens of social groups (The Sociology Writing Group, 2008). Edwards (2012) notes that sociologists may start inquiring about an individual's behavior but then "go bigger", questioning how small groups or larger organizations and social structures shape that behavior. Mr. Huaqui questioned whether economic differences exist at comparable occupational prestige levels across race. To answer this question, he analyzed data from one of the most common databases in social science: The General Social Survey (GSS; National Opinion Research Center, 2008). This report is formatted in ASA style (ASA, 2010) and illustrates the five-finger Humanoid structure.

SAMPLE PAPER

Prestige Isn't Everything: Racial Differences in Economic Attainment Despite Comparable Occupational Prestige
Anthony Huaqui
Central Connecticut State University

Abstract
This paper examines how race moderates the relationship between occupational prestige and economic attainment. Data from the 2008 General Social Survey were analyzed. Although racial minorities have lower occupational prestige than whites, the effect is quite small. Racial minorities are more likely than whites to attribute economic disparity to race at all levels of prestige, but especially at low levels of prestige. Whites are more likely to own homes than racial minorities at all levels of occupational prestige and particularly at moderate levels of prestige. Race and occupational prestige predict unique portions of variation in income. However, race and occupational prestige do not significantly interact to predict income.

Taken together, these findings partially support the conclusion that race is a stronger predictor of economic attainment than occupational prestige. For some indicators, occupational prestige moderates the relationship between race and economic attainment.

Introduction

How worthy is your job perceived by society? Is such worthiness rewarded economically? According to a recent Harris poll of over 2,000 adults in the United States (The Harris Poll 2014), the most prestigious occupations include physicians, military officers, firefighters, scientists, and nurses. Nevertheless, in the same poll, parents were most likely to encourage their children to become engineers – a career with less prestige than the aforementioned professions. Why?

Parental attitudes are mirroring the fact that occupational prestige does not actually measure the economic attainment of occupations. Prestige is strictly a measure of the perceived social value attributed to a job. The National Opinion Research Center (NORC) first started measuring occupational prestige in the 1940s to identify social status associated with professions (Duncan 1961). Occupational prestige has been measured regularly as part of the General Social Survey since the 1970s (The General Social Survey 2014) and has remained extremely stable over decades (Nakao and Treas 1994). However, more recent data show generational differences in perceived prestige (The Harris Poll 2014).

From a conceptual standpoint, occupational prestige is not the best indicator of economic attainment. Nevertheless, occupational prestige may mitigate income inequality related to demographic factors, particularly race. To test this hypothesis, I examine whether occupational prestige moderates the relationship between race and income, as indexed by home ownership and yearly income. Further, I investigate whether occupational prestige plays a role in people's perceptions of economic inequality due to race. I contend that occupational prestige partially mitigates economic inequality across races, but it does not erase it.

REVIEW OF THE LITERATURE

Dual labor market theory posits that the labor market is split across groups of workers with differing incomes for the same work (Lemelle 2002) and may explain differences in economic attainment across whites and racial minorities (Hirsch 1980). It is clear that whites attain higher economic status than racial minorities. Xu and Leffler (1992) reported that racial minorities earn less than whites.

Other researchers examine economic inequality across race using economic indicators other than income. Smith and Elliott (2002) examined whether ethnic concentrations in occupations and industries influence how people different races attain positions of authority. Workplace authority gives access to other social benefits allocated through the labor market, such as higher pay, medical benefits, pensions, etc. In general, whites are more likely to attain supervisory positions than nonwhites. However, ethnic concentration is related to the attainment of supervisory positions to minorities. If the ethnic concentration is in entry-level workers, then the ethnic minority likely supervises entry-level workers (a basic supervisory role). Conversely, if the ethnic concentration is at higher-level positions, the ethnic minority has a greater chance to obtain a higher-level supervisory role managing upper-level workers. This hypothesis is known as the "sticky floor".

In addition to economic equalities, a widening body of research documents differences in occupational prestige across race. Generally, whites have higher occupational prestige than racial minorities (Lemelle 2002; Xu and Leffer 1992). Espino and Franz (2002) report a relationship between skin color and occupational prestige. For some Hispanic groups (Mexian and Cuban, but not Puerto Rican), people with lighter skin tones tend to have jobs with higher occupational prestige. Within the health care sector, a sector with quite high occupational prestige overall, Aguirre, Wolinsky, Niederauer, Keith, and Fann (1989) found that whites have higher occupational prestige than racial minorities.

The previous literature clearly indicates racial inequality in economic attainment and in occupational prestige. However, few if any studies have examined the intersection between occupational prestige and race as predictors of economic attainment. In the present study, I replicate previous findings documenting racial differences in economic attainment and in occupational prestige. Using data from the most recent General Social Survey, I examine two indicators of economic attainment including yearly income and home ownership. In addition to examining economic attainment, the GSS offers the unique possibility of investigating beliefs explaining economic disparity. Specifically, I examine whether occupational prestige moderates the relationship between race and belief that income inequality is due to racial discrimination. Consistent with dual market labor theory, I expect whites to report higher levels of economic attainment and occupational prestige than racial differences. Further, racial differences should attribute economic disparity due to racial discrimination more strongly than whites. This pattern may be especially evident at lower levels of prestige, in accordance with the "sticky floor" hypothesis (Smith and Elliott 2002). Finally, I probe whether race, occupational prestige, or the interaction between the two explain variation in yearly income.

METHODS
Data
I used responses from the 2008 General Social Survey (GSS; National Opinion Research Center, 2008) to address my research question. Since 1972, the General Social Survey has collected data on various social factors from community-dwelling adults in the continental United States. The 2008 General Social Survey contained 2023 respondents.

Measures
The following variables were used in this study: RACE (Race of Respondent), PRESTG80 (Respondent's Occupational Prestige Score [1980]), RINCOM06 (Respondent's Income), DWELOWN (Does Respondent Own or Rent Home), and RACDIF1 (Economic Differences Due to Discrimination). The independent variables were RACE and PRESTG80. The dependent variables were RINCOM06, DWELOWN, and RACDIF1.

Methods
First, I used an analysis of variance to examine whether respondents' race (RACE) is related to their occupational prestige (PRESTG80). To increase statistical power, I recoded RACE into two categories: whites ($n = 1559$) and racial minorities ($n = 464$). I expect whites to report having jobs with higher occupational prestige than minorities.

Second, I used a multivariate cross-tabulation with a chi-square test of independence to investigate whether racial minorities high in occupational prestige are more likely that whites to believe that racial differences in wealth indictors are due to discrimination. The recoded RACE acts as the independent variable. PRESTG80 functions as the control variable; I recoded PRESTG80 into a three-level categorical variable of occupational prestige: low ($n = 750$), moderate ($n = 638$), and high ($n = 635$). RACDIF1, a binary response, acts as the dependent variable. I predict that racial minorities at all levels of prestige are more likely to believe there are economic differences between whites and racial minorities in the United States because of racial discrimination.

An additional multivariate cross-tabulation table with chi-square test of independence will evaluate whether racial minorities with high occupational prestige are less likely to own homes. Again, recoded RACE is the independent variable and recoded PRESTG80 is the control variable. However the dependent variable is DWELOWN. The original variable contains three categories: "Own or Is Buying", "Rent", and "Other". However, I will combine "Rent" and "Other" into a single category because the sample size of "Other" was comparatively small. Thus, 889 respondents are classified as "Own or Is Buying" and 438 respondents are categorized as "Rent or Other". Of note, 696 people did not respond to this question. I hypothesize that whites with high occupational prestige are more likely to own homes than racial minorities with high occupational prestige.

The final analysis is a multiple regression with moderation to examine whether racial minorities with high occupational prestige earn less than whites with high occupational prestige. The original PRESTG80 variable and RACE are predictors; RINCOM06 acts as the outcome variable. To create an interaction term PRESTG80*RACE, I centered PRESTG80 and then multiplied this variable by RACE. I predict that occupational prestige will predict increases in income. Further, I expect that racial minorities, regardless of occupational prestige will earn less income that whites. It is unclear whether occupational prestige and race will interact to explain variation in income.

ANALYSIS AND INTERPRETATION OF FINDINGS
Hypothesis 1

Respondents' race was significantly associated with occupational prestige, $F(1, 1119) = 14.58$, $p < .001$, $\eta_p^2 = .008$. Although whites reported significantly more occupational prestige ($M = 44.43$, $SD = 13.81$) than racial minorities ($M = 41.55$, $SD = 13.95$), the effect size was extremely low. Race explains approximately 1% of the variation in occupational prestige scores between whites and racial minorities.

Hypothesis 2

As illustrated in Figure 1, the three variables of race, occupational prestige, and belief that racial differences fuel economic disparity were significantly and moderately associated, $\chi^2(1, N = 1274) = 49.93$, $p < .001$, Cramer's $v = .198$. For each level of occupational prestige, racial minorities were more likely to believe that racial discrimination caused economic disparity [$6.20 \leq \chi^2 \leq 29.41$, all p's $< .017$, $.128 \leq$ Cramer's $v \leq .248$]. The racial difference was most pronounced at low occupational prestige, with approximately 27% more racial minorities than whites espousing the belief. However, at high occupational prestige, this difference declined to just shy of 16%. Of note, at low occupational prestige more than the majority of racial minorities (61.9%) believed that racial discrimination created economic inequity. However, only 43.5% of racial minorities with high occupational prestige shared this belief. This analysis suggests that race interacts with occupational prestige to shape beliefs about economic attainment.

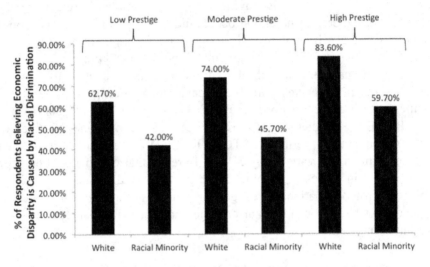

Figure 1. The interaction between race and occupational prestige for belief that economic disparity is due to racial discrimination

Hypothesis 3

Figure 2 illustrates the interaction between race and occupational prestige and actual economic attainment, as indicated by home ownership. Race, occupational prestige, and home ownership were significantly and moderately associated, $\chi^2(1, N = 1327) = 72.42, p < .001$, Cramer's $v = .234$. For each level of occupational prestige, whites were more likely to own or be in the processing of buying a home than racial minorities [$17.53 \leq \chi^2 \leq 28.687$, all p's $< .001$, $.187 \leq$ Cramer's $v \leq .234$]. Whereas the percentage of whites owning homes increased almost 22% as a function of occupational prestige, the percentage of racial minorities owning homes increased only 18%. Further, the greatest disparity across race emerged at moderate levels of occupational prestige: whites were more than one-third more likely to own a home than racial minorities.

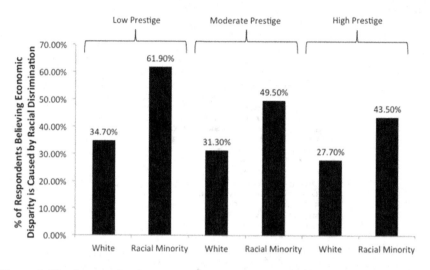

Figure 2. The interaction between race and prestige for home ownership

Hypothesis 4

I conducted a multiple regression to examine whether occupational prestige, race, and the interaction between prestige and race predicted unique variation in income. Because income was negatively skewed, I applied a square root transformation on the reversed scores. The values from the regression model reflect the transformed scores, whereas Figure 3 depicts original values.

The overall regression model was statistically significant, $F(3, 1185) = 87.09$, $p < .001$, and accounted for approximately 17.9% of the variation in income. As expected, whites earned more than racial minorities, $\beta = -0.12$, $t(1187) = -4.40$, $p < .001$. The part correlation indicates that approximately 11.6% of the variation in income can be explained by race alone. Further, people with higher occupational prestige earned more than people with low occupational prestige, $\beta = 0.27$, $t(1187) = 3.40$, $p = .001$. Approximately 8.9% of the variation in income was uniquely explained by occupational prestige. Although the interaction between race and occupational prestige was not significant, $\beta = 0.13$, $t(1187) = 1.65$, $p = .098$, Figure 3 suggests a trend consistent with other analyses that the greatest impact of race occurs at lower levels of occupational prestige. Thus, at higher levels of occupational prestige there appears to be less income disparity between whites and racial minorities.

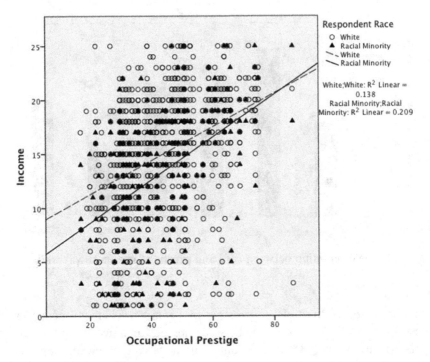

Figure 3. The relationship between occupational prestige and income for Whites and racial minorities

SUMMARY AND CONCLUSIONS

Although whites reported more occupational prestige than racial minorities, the effect size in this sample was surprisingly small (<1%). Sampling differences may explain this result. I used the General Social Survey database. Xu and Leffer's (1992) sample was derived from Baltimore, which may not represent national trends. Although Lemelle (2002) used a national database (Census Bureau Integrated Use Microdata), he did not report effect sizes and divided his analysis by race as well as biological sex.

Occupational prestige moderated the relationship between race and economic attainment differentially across outcome measures. Beliefs about economic disparity offered the clearest picture of the mitigating role of occupational prestige. At low levels of prestige, the belief that economic disparity was due to racial discrimination was moderately stronger for racial minorities than for whites. However, this relationship weakened dramatically as occupational prestige increased.

For more tangible economic indicators, the mitigating role of occupational prestige was less clear. With respect to home ownership, whites were more likely to own homes than racial minorities and this disparity was greatest at moderate levels of prestige. Perhaps racial minorities do not feel comfortable committing to a home investment until they reach higher levels of occupational prestige. Alternatively, racial minorities with moderate levels of occupational prestige may be less likely to be approved for a mortgage than whites with comparable levels of prestige. Although lending practices for Black people improved over the 1990s, Black people were still more than 2 times likely to be turned down for a mortgage than their white counterparts (Phillips, 2003). Note that the data for the present study were collected in 2008 before the subprime lending collapse. The data from the 2018 GSS may reveal greater racial disparity in home ownership with less mitigation by occupational prestige.

I observed no moderating effect of occupational prestige on the relationship between race and overall income. Although there was a trend suggesting that occupational prestige mitigated racial income inequality at higher levels of prestige, the interaction was not statistically significant. Even if the interaction achieved statistical significance, it would account for very little variation in income.

Several limitations qualify these conclusions. First, for some variables, there was substantial missing data. For example, 1327 out of 2023 possible respondents reported home ownership. Further, 1274 out of 2023 possible respondents answered questions about economic disparity being due to racial discrimination. Thus, the sample may not be truly representative of the general population. Second, there are two important factors that I did not control for in these analyses: biological sex and educational attainment. Clearly, an income gap exists between men and women and this gap differs across race. Although educational attainment is associated with occupational prestige (more prestigious jobs such as physicians and scientists require many years of schooling), the relationship is not perfect. Future research should use a broader sample to adequately account for these variables. Third, the overall trends reported in the present paper are for a cross-section of the entire United States. The moderating effect of occupational prestige on the relationship between race and economic attainment may manifest differently across regions of the United States that differ in their beliefs and display of racial discrimination. Finally, because of statistical power considerations, all racial minorities were grouped together. The relationship between race and other variables observed in this study may differ across specific racial and ethnic groups.

Clearly, inequality in occupational prestige and economic attainment still exists in the United States. Nevertheless, these findings suggest that occupational prestige partially moderates the relationship between race and economic attainment. Not surprisingly, the greatest inequality exists at the lowest levels of prestige. Enhancing opportunities to attain positions with greater occupational prestige may help reduce economic disparities across race.

References

Aguirre, Benigno E., Fredric D. Wolinsky, John Niederauer, Verna Keith, and Lih-Jiuan Fann. 1989. "Occupational Prestige in the Health Care Delivery System." *Journal of Health and Social Behavior,* 30:315–29.

Duncan, Otis D. 1961. "A Socioeconomic Index for All Occupations." Pp. 109–38 in *Occupations and Social Status*, edited by Albert J. Reiss, Jr. New York: Free Press.

Espino, Rodolfo and Michael M. Franz. 2002. "Latino Phenotypic Discrimination Revisited: The Impact of Skin Color on Occupational Status." *Social Sciences Quarterly,* 83(2):612–23.

Hirsch, Eric. 1980. "Dual Labor Market Theory: A Sociological Critique." *Sociological Inquiry*, 50(2):133–45.

Lamelle, Anthony. 2002. "The Effects of the Intersection of Race, Gender, and Educational Class on Occupational Prestige." *The Western Journal of Black Studies*, 26(2):89–97.

Nakao, Keiko and Judith Treas. 1994. "Updating Occupational Prestige and Socioeconomic Scores: How the New Measures Measure Up." Pp. 1–72 in *Sociological Methodology*, edited by Peter Marsden. Washington, DC: American Sociological Association.

Phillips, Sandra. 2003. "African Americans and Mortgage Lending Discrimination". *The Western Journal of Black Studies*, 27(2):65–79.

Smith, Ryan A. and James R. Elliot. 2002. "Does Ethnic Concentration Influence Employees' Access to Authority? An Examination of Contemporary Urban Labor Markets." *Social Forces,* 81(1):255–79.

The General Social Survey. 2014. "About the GSS". Chicago. Retrieved March 2, 2016 (http://gss.norc.org/About-The-GSS)

The Harris Poll. 2014. "Doctors, Military Officers, Firefighters, and Scientists Seen as Among America's Most Prestigious Occupations". September 10. New York: Retrieved March 14, 2016 (http://www.theharrispoll.com/politics/ Doctors__Military_Officers__Firefighters__and_Scientists_Seen_as_ Among_America_s_Most_Prestigious_Occupations.html)

Xu, Wu, and Ann Leffler. 1992. "Gender and Race Effects on Occupational Prestige, Segregation, and Earnings". *Gender & Society*, 6(3):376–92.

CHAPTER 11

PRIMARY DATA COLLECTION

INTRODUCTION

Ms. Selina Nieves collected data from other undergraduates for her study in Psychological Science. Psychological scientists examine behaviors, cognitions, and emotions with the goal of understanding how humans experience the world. Emerging researchers in criminology, communications, and behavioral economics often take a psychological approach in posing and answering research questions. Ms. Nieves compared men and women's liking for happy and sad musical excerpts after being placed in a sad mood. Her study illustrates a true experimental manipulation and also contains published self-report measures. Consequently, you will see how to describe stimuli as well as questionnaires. Further, this research report contains excellent examples of secondary analyses, including manipulation checks. The paper is formatted in APA style (APA, 2010) and illustrates the four-finger Simpson structure.

SAMPLE PAPER

Mood and Music: Sex Differences In Music-Liking Under Sad-Mood
Induction
Selina Nieves
Central Connecticut State University

Abstract

Research has well established that music modulates people's mood. More recent research has demonstrated that the relationship between mood and music is bidirectional: people's mood affects their musical preferences. Although people generally gravitate towards liking happy music, people who are in a sad mood increase their liking for sad music. Given documented sex differences in emotional responsiveness and general mood, I compared men's and women's preferences for happy- and sad-sounding music after putting them in a sad mood. People in a sad mood liked sad music more than they liked happy music, $p < .001$, $\eta_p^2 = .826$. Further, men and women provided comparable likeability for happy and sad music, $p = .810$, $\eta_p^2 = .002$. Regardless of biological sex, misery loves company.

Mood and Music: Sex Differences In Music-Liking Under Sad-Mood Induction

Researchers have consistently demonstrated that listening to music affects mood. For example, people's emotional responses to music are consistent with the emotions suggested by structural features of the music (Hunter, Schellenberg, & Schimmack, 2010). Happy music in a major mode with a fast tempo elicits a pleasant mood whereas sad music in a minor mode with a slow tempo promotes an unpleasant mood. However, less research has examined whether mood affects people's music preferences. Listening to happy music when one is happy makes intuitive sense. But why would anyone who is already feeling sad want to listen to something that is sad? Further, it is unclear whether individual differences associated with emotional processing moderate such an effect. The overarching purpose of the current study is to compare preferences for sad music in men and women who have been induced to feel sad.

Seeking out music that is congruent with one's mood has parallels with mood congruency effects observed in memory and attention. Negative moods increases attention to negative words and images compared to positive words and images (Isaacowitz, Toner, Goren, & Wilson, 2008). Further, clinical depression biases attention towards negatively valenced stimuli (Maat, Vásquez, & Campbell, 1992).

Although people generally prefer happy music, their liking of sad music increases when they feel sad. Hunter, Schellenberg, and Griffith (2011) demonstrated that inducing a sad mood caused people to like happy and sad music comparably. However, individual differences in emotional processing and regulation may moderate that effect.

Emotional responses to music are stronger in women than in men (Panskepp, 1995). Further, women tend to express negative moods more often than men and even appear to enjoy dwelling in a depressed state (Nolen-Hoeksema, 1990; Butler & Nolen-Hoeksema, 1994). Butler and Nolen-Hoeksema (1994) reported that 92% of women compared to 46% of men chose to engage in an emotion-related task that prolonged their sad mood rather than distracting themselves.

Thus, the purpose of the present study is to examine whether sex differences moderate preference for happy or sad songs while feeling sad. Women and men viewed images to induce sadness and then rated their liking for happy and sad musical excerpts. Consistent with Hunter et al. (2011), I expected that people would not exhibit the typical bias towards happy music and instead like both happy and sad music comparably. Given that women respond more strongly to emotional stimuli than do men (Fujita, Deiner, & Sandvik, 1991; Grossman & Wood, 1993; Kring & Gordon, 1998), I predicted that women's liking for emotionally valanced music would be stronger than men's liking. Finally, I hypothesized that biological sex would moderate the relationship between mood and music. Women should exhibit stronger preferences for sad music than men, given women's tendency to make choices that prolong a sad state (Butler & Nolen-Hoeksema, 1994).

Method

Participants

The sample consisted of 40 undergraduates (21 females, 19 males) from a Northeastern regional public university. Students received course credit for their participation. Participants were between 18 and 25 years of age ($M = 20.00$ years, $SD = 1.89$). The majority of participants (62.5%) identified as non-Hispanic Caucasians and racial/ethnic identification did not differ across men and women, $\chi^2(4, 40) = 0.78$, $p = .942$, Cramer's $v = .139$.

All participants reported having good hearing and eyesight. Over half of the sample (60%) reported having some musical training: 1–3 years ($n = 6$), 4–5 years ($n = 4$), and 6+ years ($n = 7$). Seven participants did not report the duration of their musical training.

Materials

Demographics questionnaire. Participants reported their age, biological sex, race and ethnicity, and answered questions about their student status (e.g., total number of credits, cumulative GPA, extracurricular activities). Further, participants described their previous musical training, which I defined as knowing how to read music or being involved in activities where you would have to know how to read music and understand music concepts, such as tempo. Participants confirmed that they had normal hearing and were wearing corrective lenses if applicable (see Appendix A).

Postitive and Negative Affect Schedule (PANAS; Watson, Clark, & Tellegen, 1998). This self-report scale consists of 20 items measuring positive (e.g., alert) and negative (e.g., afraid) affect. Respondents rated how each word described their current momentary mood using 5-point scale from 1 (*very slightly or not at all*) to 5 (*extremely*). Both positive and negative subscales exhibited adequate inter-item consistency (Cronbach's α = .89, Cronbach's α = .85; see Appendix B).

Sad mood induction. To induce a sad mood, participants viewed Hunter et al.'s (2011) stimuli consisting of 12 color images depicting sad content (e.g., injured animals). Each picture was sized to fill a PowerPoint slide. Brief written descriptions appeared under each image (e.g., "injured turtle") to emphasize negative affect. Using a Direct RT script (Empirisoft, 2012), images appeared on the computer screen in a random order for 15 seconds each. Participants rated each image on a 7-point bipolar sad-happy rating scale using the computer's keypad. Responses ranged from 0 (*extremely sad*) to 6 (*extremely happy*). Upon making a response, the next image appeared until participants rated all 12 images. Then participants selected one of the images and wrote a reflective statement about it for 2 minutes (see Appendix C).

Musical excerpts. Participants listened to six 30-second musical excerpts. Five selections were from Hunter et al.'s (2011) stimuli that derived from commercial recordings in an assortment of musical styles. I provided the sixth excerpt. Excerpts were presented though headphones at equal volume (see Appendix D).

Procedure

This study received institutional IRB approval. I conducted my study in a small computer lab testing up to 5 participants at a time. Each participant sat at his or her own computer terminal. Dividers were placed between terminals for privacy. I informed participants that the purpose of my study was to examine the relationship between mood and music. Participants then read and signed the informed consent.

Participants completed the demographics questionnaire and the PANAS. Next, they experienced the sad mood induction. As a manipulation check, participants completed the PANAS again. Then I instructed participants to put on their headphones to listen to six short musical excerpts. After listening to each excerpt, participants answered three questions: "How much did you LIKE the music?", "How happy or sad did the music SOUND?", and "How familiar did the music SOUND?" Consistent with Hunter et al. (2011), participants recorded responses on a 7-point scale (0 to 6).

To minimize the impact of the sad mood induction, participants experienced Hunter et al.'s (2011) happy mood induction by viewing images and reflecting on of them. After participants completed the induction, I distributed a written debriefing informing them that I was examining sex differences in responses to happy and sad music while in a sad mood. The procedure lasted approximately 20 minutes.

Results

Sad Mood Induction

Image ratings. To confirm that participants found the images sad, I averaged ratings across the 12 images. Ratings ($M = 1.04$, $SD = 0.70$, 95% CI [0.82, 1.27]) were significantly below the neutral threshold of 3.00, $t(39) = 17.78$, $p < .001$, Cohen's $d = 2.81$. Although women ($M = 0.90$, $SD = 0.59$, 95% CI [0.63, 1.17]) found the images more sad on average than did men ($M = 1.20$, $SD = 0.78$, 95% CI [0.82, 1.58]), this difference was not statistically significant, $t(38) = 1.38$, $p = .175$, Cohen's $d = 0.43$.

Mood. I examined whether participants' mood changed after experiencing the sad mood induction. Although negative affect scores on the PANAS were positively skewed, the change in negative affect was normally distributed for both men and women. I conducted a 2 × 2 mixed-model MANOVA with time (pre-induction, post-induction) as a within-participant factor and biological sex (male, female) as a between-participants factor. Sums of positive and negative affect scores were the dependent variables. Positive affect significantly decreased after induction ($M_{pre} = 29.97$, $SD = 9.69$; $M_{post} = 25.33$, $SD = 9.76$), $F(1, 38) = 29.57$, $p < .001$, $\eta^2_p = .438$. Conversely, negative affect significantly increased after induction ($M_{pre} = 13.85$, $SD = 4.52$; $M_{post} = 15.98$, $SD = 5.91$), $F(1, 38) = 7.87$, $p = .008$, $\eta^2_p = .172$. Neither the main effect of biological sex nor the interaction between biological sex and time were statistically significant for positive or negative affect scores (all p's > .174). Thus, the sad mood induction effectively changed participants' mood and was comparably salient for men and women.

Primary Analysis

To evaluate whether men and women differed in their liking of the happy and sad excerpts, I conducted a 2 × 2 mixed-model ANOVA with valence (happy, sad) as a within-participant factor and biological sex (male, female) as a between-participants factor. Findings are illustrated in Figure 1.Contrary to prediction, participants vastly preferred sad music to happy music, $F(1, 38) = 88.24$, $p < .001$, $\eta^2_p = .699$. I observed no main effect of biological

151

sex, $F(1, 38) = 1.420$, $p = .241$, $\eta^2_p = .036$ or interaction between biological sex and valence, $F(1, 38) = 0.018$, $p = .894$, $\eta^2_p < .001$.

Secondary Analyses

Affect ratings for musical excerpts. Following the approach of the primary analysis, I conducted a 2 × 2 mixed-model ANOVA to evaluate whether participants reliably identified the intended valence of the musical excerpts. Participants rated happy excerpts ($M = 3.33$, $SD = 0.47$) significantly more positively than sad excerpts ($M = 0.93$, $SD = 0.83$), $F(1, 38) = 179.93$, $p < .001$, $\eta^2_p = .83$. Ratings appeared comparable across biological sex, $F(1, 38) = 0.07$, $p = .800$, $\eta^2_p = .070$ and there was no interaction between biological sex and affect, $F(1, 38) = 0.06$, $p = .810$, $\eta^2_p < .001$.

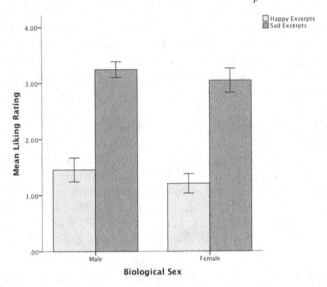

Figure 1. Mean liking ratings for happy and sad musical excerpts across men and women. Error bars represent ± 1 SE.

Familiarity ratings for musical excerpts. To compare familiarity ratings for happy and sad excerpts across men and women, I conducted a 2 × 2 mixed-model ANOVA. I observed a statistically significant interaction between biological sex and affect, $F(1, 38) = 5.97$, $p = .019$, $\eta^2_p = .140$. Familiarity ratings for happy songs were comparable across men ($M = 2.39$, $SD = 0.69$) and women ($M = 2.70$, $SD = 0.71$). However, men reported greater familiarity with sad songs ($M = 1.23$, $SD = 0.96$) than did women ($M = 0.67$, $SD = 0.64$).

Discussion

In the current study, I compared men's and women's liking of happy and sad music while they were in a sad mood. Whereas Hunter and colleagues (2011) found that inducing a sad mood produced comparable liking ratings for happy and sad excerpts, I found that participants who felt sad preferred sad music to happy music by more than a factor of 2. Further, I found no differences in music liking or emotional processing between women and men.

Why did participants in my study vastly prefer sad music to happy music while in a sad mood? Participants in my sample may have been music empathizers who viewed music as emotional communication (Kreutz, Schubert, & Mitchell, 2008). By contrast, music systematizers take a more analytical approach to music listening. Future research should examine whether preference for sad music while sad is associated with musical listening style.

The testing situation may also explain the current results. Hunter et al. (2011) tested participants individually; I tested participants in groups. Perhaps emotional contagion occurred in my study. In emotional contagion, people perceive others' emotional behavior and unconsciously replicate it. The act of replicating emotional behavior causes people to feel that behavior themselves, presumably through the action of the mirror neuron system (Dezecache, Jacob, & Grèzes, 2015). Although participants in my study listened to music through headphones and partitions were placed between computer stations, participants could still see each other. Perhaps participants perceived others' body language and facial expressions, increasing the salience of the mood induction and subsequent liking for sad music.

Despite evidence suggesting that women respond more strongly to emotional stimuli than do men (e.g., Fujita et al., 1991; Grossman & Wood, 1993; Panskepp, 1995) and that women tend to make choices to prolong a sad state (Butler & Nolen-Hoeksema, 1994), I observed no sex differences in music liking or emotional processing. The images and musical excerpts in the present study were gender neutral. Using stimuli that activates gender schemas may produce differences in people who identify strongly with a particular gender and corresponding stereotypes.

The current findings have implications for music therapy. Masumoto (2002) reported that deeply sad participants felt less sad after listening to sad music. Although participants in the current study were not "deeply sad", the current findings suggest that people like emotional stimuli that matches their current mood. The act of matching behavior to current cognitions and emotions may reduce cognitive dissonance and improve mood.

My findings add to the literature on mood congruency in the musical domain (Hunter et al., 2010; Hunter et al., 2011). Men and women appear to exhibit comparable mood congruency for music. The particularly strong effect of liking sad music while in a sad mood observed in the present study may be due to empathizing deeply with music or experiencing emotional contagion. Misery may indeed love company.

References

Butler, L. D., & Nolen-Hoeksema, S. (1994). Gender differences in responses to depressed mood in a college sample. *Sex Roles, 30,* 331–346. doi:10.1007/BF01420597

Dezecache, G., Jacob, P., & Grèzes, J. (2015) Emotional contagion: Its scope and limitations. *Trends in Cognitive Sciences, 19,* 297–299. doi: 10.1016/j.tics.2015.03.011

DirectRT (Version 2012) [Computer software]. New York, NY: Empirisoft Corporation

Fujita, F., Diener, E., & Sandvik, E. (1991). Gender differences in negative affect and well-being: The case for emotional intensity. *Journal of Personality and Social Psychology, 61,* 427–434.

Grossman, M., & Wendy Wood, W. (1993). Sex differences in intensity of emotional experience: A social role interpretation. *Journal of Personality and Social Psychology, 65,* 1010–1022.

Hunter, P. G., Schellenberg, E., & Griffith, A. T. (2011). Misery loves company: Mood-congruent emotional responding to music. *Emotion, 11,* 1068–1072. doi:10.1037/a0023749

Hunter, P. G., Schellenberg, E., & Schimmack, U. (2008). Mixed affective responses to music with conflicting cues. *Cognition and Emotion, 22,* 327–352.doi:10.1080/02699930701438145.

Hunter, P. G., Schellenberg, E., & Schimmack, U. (2010). Feelings and perceptions of happiness and sadness induced by music: Similarities, differences, and mixed emotions. *Psychology of Aesthetics, Creativity, and the Arts, 4,* 47–56. doi:10.1037/a0016873.

Isaacowitz, D. M., Toner, K., Goren, D., & Wilson, H. R. (2008). Looking while unhappy: Mood-congruent gaze in young adults, positive gaze in older adults. *Psychological Science, 19,* 848–853.

Kring, A. M., & Gordon, A. H. (1998). Sex differences in emotion: Expression, experience, and physiology. *Journal of Personality and Social Psychology, 74*(3), 686–703. doi:10.1037/0022-3514.74.3.686

Matsumoto, J. (2002). Why people listen to sad music: Effects of music on sad moods. *Japanese Journal of Educational Psychology, 50*(1), 23–32.

Matt, G. E., Vázquez, C., & Campbell, W. K. (1992). Mood-congruent recall of affectively toned stimuli: A meta-analytic review. *Clinical Psychology Review, 12,* 227–255.

Nolen-Hoeksema, S. (1990). *Sex differences in depression.* Stanford University Press.

Panksepp, J. (1995). The emotional sources of 'chills' induced by music. *Music Perception, 13*, 171–207.

Watson, D., Clark, L., & Tellegen, A. (1988). Development and Validation of Brief Measures of Positive and Negative Affect: The PANAS Scales. *Journal of Personality and Social Psychology, 54*, 1063–1070.

JOURNEY'S END... OR IS IT?

Well, emerging researcher, you've been on quite a wild ride. Take a moment to ponder all you have accomplished. Developing a research question, formulating and implementing a methodology, and analyzing the data stretched your creativity, judgment, and perspective. But these feats, notable as they are, pale in comparison to writing your report.

Think about it. You introduced readers to your research question by hooking them, contextualizing your question with extant research and theory, and convincing readers why your question was worth studying. You described how you went about answering your question in a way that others could replicate. You described what you found and supported your conclusions with a second language – statistics. You considered alternative explanations for your findings, critically examined limitations, discussed potential applications of your research, and – again – made readers care about your work. You wrangled with seemingly countless formatting rules. And, to top it off, you revised and reworked your prose to make it accessible to the widest audience. Wow.

Should your journey end here? It can, but it doesn't have to. In writing your quantitative research report, you have made yourself part of something much grander than you probably realized. You have become a member of the scientific community. Scientists not only conduct research, they share their research with anyone willing to listen or read. Would you present your research at a local, regional, or national conference? Is your work publishable in a scholarly outlet? Could you write a blog about your research?

Carl Sagan noted, "We live in a society dependent on science and technology, in which hardly anyone knows anything about science and technology." As the next generation of social and behavioral scientists, you have the opportunity to change that. Take a step in that direction by partnering with your professor and taking your research report to the next level. Communicate your research so that you can push science *and* society forward.

REFERENCES

Aftermath of an unfounded vaccine scare. (2013, May 22). *The New York Times.* Retrieved from http://nyti.ms/1xXWlkV

Ahn, W.-Y., Kishida, K. T., Gu, X., Lohrenz, T. Harvey, A., Alford, J. R., Smith, K. B., Yaffe, G., Hibbing, J. R., Dayan, P., & Montague, P. R. (2014). Nonpolitical images evoke naural predictors of political ideology. *Current Biology, 24,* 2693–2699. doi:10.1016/j.cub.2014.09.050

American Political Science Association Committee of Publications. (2006). *APSA style manual for political science.* Washington, DC: American Political Science Association. Retrieved from www.apsanet.org

American Psychological Association. (2010). *Publication manual of the American Psychological Association* (6th ed.). Washington, DC: American Psychological Association.

American Sociological Association. (2010). *American Sociological Association style guide* (4th ed.). Washington, DC: American Sociological Assocation.

Ames, D. R., Rose, P., & Anderson, C. P. (2006). The NPI-16 as a short measure of narcissism. *Journal of Research in Personality, 40,* 440–450. doi:10.1016/j.jrp.2005.03.002

Bain, K. (2004). *What the best college teachers do.* Cambridge, MA: Harvard University Press.

Becker, H. S. (2007). *Writing for social scientists: How to start and finish your thesis, book, or article* (2nd ed.). Chicago, IL: University of Chicago Press.

Bem, D. J. (2004). Writing the empirical article. In J. M. Darley, M. P. Zanna, & H. L. Roediger III (Eds.), *The compleat academic: A career guide* (2nd ed.). Washington, DC: American Psychological Association.

Blackwell, L. S., Trzeniewski, K. H., & Dweck, C. S. (2007). Implicit theories of intelligence predict achievement across an adolescent transition: A longitudinal student and an intervention. *Child Development, 78,* 246–263.

Boice, R. (1990). Faculty resistance to writing-intensive courses. *Teaching of Psychology, 17,* 13–17.

Bonaccio, S., & Reeve, C. L. (2010). The nature and relative importance of students' perceptions of the sources of test anxiety. *Learning and Individual Differences, 20,* 617–625. doi:10.1016/j.lindif.2010.09.007

Bransford, J. D., & Johnson, M. K. (1972). Contextual prerequisites for understanding: Some investigations of comprehension and recall. *Journal of Verbal Learning and Verbal Behavior, 11,* 717–726.

Brown, P. C., Roediger, III, H. L., & McDaniel, M. A. (2014). *Make it stick: The science of successful learning.* Cambridge, MA: Harvard University Press.

Cohen, J. (1992). A power primer. *Psychological Bulletin, 112,* 155–159.

Creswell, J. W. (2014). *Research design: Qualitative, quantitative, and mixed methods approaches* (4th ed.). Washington, DC: Sage.

Csikszentmihalyi, M. (1996). *Creativity: Flow and the psychology of discovery and invention.* New York, NY: Harper Perennial.

Cumming, G. (2013). *Understanding the new statistics: Effect sizes, confidence intervals, and meta-analysis.* New York, NY: Routledge.

Cumming, G. (2014). The new statistics: Why and how. *Psychological Science, 25,* 7–29. doi:10.1177/0956797613504966

Cumming, G., & Finch, S. (2005). Inference by eye: Confidence intervals and how to read pictures of data. *American Psychologist, 60,* 170–180. doi:10.1037/0003-066X.60.2.170

Dominus, S. (2011, April 20). The crash and burn of an autism guru. *The New York Times Magazine.* Retrieved from http://nyti.ms/1BEMWnr

Doucleff, M. (2014, June 2). Anatomy of a dance hit: Why we love to boogie with Pharrell [Radio broadcast]. *Health Shots.* Washington, DC: National Public Radio. Retrieved from http://www.npr.org/sections/health-shots/2014/05/30/317019212/anatomy-of-a-dance-hit-why-we-love-to-boogie-with-pharrell

Duckworth, A. L., Peterson, C., Matthews, M. D., & Kelly, D. R. (2007). Grit: Perseverance and passion for long-term goals. *Journal of Personality and Social Psychology, 9,* 1087–1101.

Dunn, D. S. (2004). *A short guide to writing about Psychology.* New York, NY: Pearson Longman.

Dweck, C. S. (2006). *Mindset: The new psychology of success.* New York, NY: Ballantine.

Edwards, M. (2012). *Writing in sociology.* Washington, DC: Sage.

Ericsson, K. A., Krampe, R. Th., & Tesch-Römer, C. (1993). The role of deliberate practice in the acquisition of expert performance. *Psychological Review, 100,* 363–406. doi:10.1037/0033-295X.100.3.363

Ferreira, F. (1991). Effects of length and syntactic complexity on initiation times for prepared utterances. *Journal of Memory and Language, 30,* 210–233. doi:10.1016/0749-596X(91)90004-4

Flower, L. (1979). Writer-based prose: A cognitive basis for problems in writing. *College English, 41,* 19–37.

Flower, L., & Hayes, J. (1977). Problem-solving strategies and the writing process. *College English, 39,* 449–461.

Goddard, T., Kahn, K. B., & Adkins, A. (2015). Racial bias in driver yielding behavior at crosswalks. *Transportation Research Part F: Traffic Psychology and Behaviour, 33,* 1–6. doi: 10.1016/j.trf.2015.06.002

Grant, H., & Dweck, C. S. (2003). Clarifying achievement goals and their impact. *Journal of Personality and Social Psychology, 85,* 541–553. doi:10.1037/0022-3514.85.3.541

Heggen, A. H. (2014). *The role of disability in Buffy the Vampire Slayer* (Unpublished doctoral dissertation). University of New Mexico, Albuquerque, NM.

Heiman, G. W. (2002). *Research methods in psychology* (3rd ed.). New York, NY: Houghton Mifflin.

Howe, M. J. A. (1999). *Genius explained.* Cambridge, United Kingdom: Cambridge University Press.

Ifcher, J., & Zarghamee, H. (2014). The happiness of single mothers: Evidence from the general social survey. *Journal of Happiness Studies, 15,* 1219–1238. doi:10.1007/s10902-013-9472-5

Kalis, P., & Neuendorf, K. A. (1989). Aggressive cue prominence and gender participant in MTV. *Journalism Quarterly, 66,* 148–154, 229.

Kendell, P. C., Silk, J. S., & Chu. B. C. (2000). Introducing your research report: Writing the introduction. In R. J. Sternberg (Ed.), *Guide to publishing in psychology journals* (pp. 41–57). New York, NY: Cambridge Univeristy Press.

Kerlinger, F. N. (1979). *Behavioral research: A conceptual approach.* New York, NY: Holt, Rinehart, & Winston.

Keyes, R. (2003). *The writer's book of hope.* New York, NY: Holt.

Kreider, R. M. (2005). *Number, timing, and duration of marriages and divorces: 2001* (Household Economics Studies). Washington, DC: U.S. Bureau of the Census. Retrieved from https://www.census.gov/prod/2005pubs/p70-97.pdf

Krippendorf, K. (2004). *Content analysis: An introduction to its methodology* (2nd ed.). Thousand Oaks, CA: Sage.

Lay, C. (1986). At last, my research article on procrastination. *Journal of Research in Personality, 20,* 474–495.

Lee, L., Frederick, S., & Ariely, D. (2006). Try it, you'll like it: The influence of expectation, consumption, and revelation on preferences for beer. *Psychological Science, 17,* 1054–1058.

Lewis, M. (2004). *Moneyball: The art of winning an unfair game.* New York, NY: W. W. Norton & Co.

Lindberg, R. (July, 2015). *Does online course enhancement contribute to learning and social connectivity?* (Unpublished Master's Thesis). Central Connecticut State University, New Britain, CT.

Lopez, S. J. (2013). *Making hope happen.* New York, NY: Atria.

Lounsbury, J. W., Fisher, L. A., Levy, J. J., & Welsh, D. P. (2009) An investigation of character strengths relation to the academic success of college students. *Individual Differences Research, 7,* 52–69.

Martin, S. P. (n.d.). *Growing evidence for a "divorce divide"? Education and martial dissolution rates in the U.S. since the 1970s* (Russell Sage Foundation Working Paper Series). Retrieved from http://www.russellsage.org/research/reports/steve-martin

Metcalfe, J., & Wiebe, D. (1987). Intuition in insight and noninsight problem solving. *Memory & Cognition, 15,* 238–246. doi:10.3758/BF03197722

Modern Language Association. (2008). *MLA style manual and guide to scholarly publishing* (3rd ed.). New York, NY: Modern Language Association of America.

Morling, B. (2015). *Research methods in psychology: Evaluating a world of information* (2nd ed.). New York, NY: W.W. Norton & Company.

Mueller, C. M., & Dweck, C. S. (1998). Praise for intelligence can undermine children's motivation and performance. *Journal of Social and Personality Psychology, 75,* 33–52. doi:10.1037/0022-3514.75.1.33

Neuendorf, K. A. (2002). *The content analysis guidebook.* Thousand Oaks, CA: Sage.

Neuman, W. L. (2011). *Social research methods: Qualitative and quantitative approaches* (7th ed.). Boston, MA: Allyn & Bacon.

Norris, M. R., Twill, S. E., & Kim, C. (2011). Smells like teen spirit: Evaluating a Midwestern teen court. *Crime and Delinquency, 57*(2), 199–221. doi:10.1177/0011128709354037

Nosek, B., Aarts, A. A., Anderson J. A., Anderson, C. J., Attridge, P. R., Attwood, A., ... Zuni, K. (2015). Estimating the reproducibility of psychological science. *Science, 349,* 943–954. doi: 10.1126/science.aac4716

Peterson, C., & Seligman, M. E. P. (2004). *Character strengths and virtues: A handbook and classification.* Washington, DC & New York, NY: American Psychological Association and Oxford University Press.

Piaget, J. (1926). *Language and thought of the child.* New York, NY: Harcourt, Brace, and World.

Privitera, G. J. (2015). *Statistics for the behavioural sciences* (2nd ed.). Thousand Oaks, CA: Sage.

Raymond, J. C. (1986). *Writing is an unnatural act.* New York, NY: Harper Collins.

Rippeyoung, P. L. F., & Noonan, M. C. (2012). Is breastfeeding truly cost free? Income consequences of breastfeeding for women. *American Sociological Review, 77,* 244–267. doi:10.1177/0003122411435477

Schwartz, B. M., Landrum, R. E., & Garung, R. A. R. (2014). *An easy guide to APA style* (2nd ed.) Washington, DC: Sage.

Seligman, M. E. P. (2006). *Learned optimism: How to change your mind and your life.* New York, NY: Vintage Books.

Shaw, J., & Porter, S. (2015). Constructing rich false memories of committing crime. *Psychological Science, 26,* 291–301. doi:10.1177/0956797614562862

Silver, N. (2012). *The signal and the noise: Why so many predictions fail – but some don't.* New York, NY: Penguin.

Silvia, P. J. (2007). *How to write a lot: A practical guide to productive academic writing.* Washington, DC: American Psychological Association.

Snyder, C. R., Sympson, S. C., Ybasco, F. C., Borders, T. F., Babyak, M. A., & Higgins, R. L. (1996). Development and validation of the state hope scale. *Journal of Personality and Social Psychology, 70,* 321–335.

Stone, D., & Heen, S. (2014). *Thanks for the feedback: The science and art of receiving feedback well (even when it is off base, unfair, poorly delivered, and frankly, you're not in the mood).* New York, NY: Penguin.

Strunk W., Jr., & White, E. B. (1999). *The elements of style* (4th ed.). Boston, MA: Longman.

Thurman, S. (2003). *The only grammar book you'll ever need: A one-stop source for every writing assignment.* Avon, MA: Adams Media.

Tough, P. (2012). *How children succeed: Grit, curiosity, and the hidden power of character.* New York, NY: Mariner Books.

VandenBos, G. R. (Ed.). (2015). *APA dictionary of psychology* (2nd ed.) Washington, DC: American Psychological Association.

van Baaren, R. B., Holland, R. W., Kawakami, K., & van Knippenberg, A. (2004). Mimicry and prosocial behaviour. *Psychological Science, 15,* 71–74.

Villanti, A. (2016, March). *Positive attitudes toward interracially and internationally adopted children.* Poster presented at the Eastern Psychological Association Annual Conference, New York, NY.

Vincent, R. C., Davis, D. K., & Boruszkowski, L. A. (1987). Sexism on MTV: The portrayal of women in rock videos. *Journalism Quarterly, 64,* 750–755, 941.

Weber, R. P. (1990). *Basic content analysis* (2nd ed.). Newbury Park, CA: Sage.

Witek, M. A. G., Clarke, E. F., Wallentin, M., Kringelback, M. L., & Vuust, P. (2014). Syncopation, body movement, and pleasure in groove music. *PLoS ONE, 10,* e0139409. doi:10.1371/journal.pone.0094446

Vygotsky, L. (1962). *Thought and language.* Cambridge, MA: MIT Press.

Zinsser, W. (1988). *Writing to learn.* New York, NY: Harper.

Zinsser, W. (2006). *On writing well: The classic guide to nonfiction.* New York, NY: Harper.

Zullow, H. M. (1991). Pessimistic rumination in popular songs and newsmagazines predict economic recession via decreased consumer optimism and spending. *Journal of Economic Psychology, 12,* 501–526. doi:10.1016/0167-4870(91)90029-S

Zullow, H. M., Oettigen, G., Peterson, C., & Seligman, M. E. P. (1988). Pessimistic explanatory style in the historical record: CAVing LBJ, presidential candidates, and East versus West Berlin. *American Psychologist, 43,* 673–682. doi:10.1037/0003-066X.43.9.673

ABOUT THE AUTHOR

Marianne Fallon, Ph.D., is an Associate Professor of Psychological Science at Central Connecticut State University and has taught undergraduate Research Methods for over 10 years. She has mentored many emerging researchers, several of whom have won local and regional research awards and have published their research. She has won the Connecticut State University Trustees Teaching Award and has twice been named a finalist for the Central Connecticut State Excellence in Teaching Award. A cognitive psychologist, Dr. Fallon conducts research in learning, memory, perception, and motivation. Her most recent research examines how developing growth mindset and character strengths help college students learn and succeed.

Printed in the United States
by Baker & Taylor Publisher Services